Perfect
Management

Your Guidebook to Managerial Success

david shelby kirk

This publication is designed to provide authoritative information in regard to the subject matter covered. It is sold with the understanding that the author is not engaged in rendering legal or professional service. If legal or other expert assistance is required, the services of a competent professional person should be sought. (Translation: I give advice in a generic environment, but only you can decide if it works for you.)

Copyright © 2018 by david shelby kirk

Other books by david shelby kirk

MVS COBOL II

VSE COBOL II

COBOL/370 for Power Programmers

COBOL for OS/390 Power Programming

CICS: A How–To for COBOL Programmers

MVS Primer

MVS for OS/390 Primer

z/OS Primer

The Bikes and I

God and I

Dedication

I dedicate this book to the managers who gave me encouragement and enlightenment, and also who freed me to walk my path and make my own mistakes, which were many. Although I learned something useful from every manager, I would like to specifically note the early few who showed me that I had the ability to succeed in the world of business: Mr. Dudley, who supervised my efforts at a service station one teenage summer; Technical Sergeant Eugene Varga (U.S. Air Force), who empowered me while a low-ranking airman to work at a much higher level and taught me the fundamentals of performance reviews; and George McDonough of Carrier Air Conditioning, who first promoted me to management and entrusted me with serious responsibilities. There were others for whom I retain high respect for their positive influence on my career: Ralph Butt of RCA, Withro Wiggins and E. P. Rogers of Mutual of New York, Christine Stahlecker of Medicare B, and Tim Sweet of Syracuse University. Did I omit anyone? I'm sure of it; my career was a rich experience, and I learned from so many.

Table of Contents

Page intentionally left blank.

"Great things in business are never done by one person. They're done by a team of people." –Steve Jobs

Preface

Welcome to my book and my view of the skills and attitude that are needed to be effective in a management/supervisory role. My guess is you're reading this book for one or more of several reasons: 1) you've recently been promoted to a management position, 2) you aspire to become a manager and wonder what managers do to "pass the time" all day while everyone else works, or 3) you work as a manager and want a refresher on the fundamentals and ideas to create a more productive work environment. Perfect! You picked the right book.

Let me expand on that. By selecting this book, you have also self-selected yourself to prepare for a career in business management. Many people (too many, unfortunately) see management as just doing whatever they were doing before being promoted, but with more pay and authority, and they never attempt to learn the job. They see the role as "telling others what to do." Horrors. Not even close.

Regrettably, one of the causes of this is that many managers promote subordinates into management roles because the subordinates were performing non-management roles quite well — but the skills don't match, and training is often minimal or non-existent. People in this position often keep using the same skills as before and never learn the new responsibilities. Still others believe that, because they know spreadsheets and can do a cost/benefit analysis, they are ready for management. Again, not even close. Read this book. You'll want to read some sections many times, especially as you encounter similar issues on the job. This book I wrote for you.

Let's begin.

We've all encountered a variety of managers, some good, some not so good, and others we couldn't even figure out. Part of that variety is because the title of *manager* requires no special training or experience. My purpose in writing this book was to share the fundamentals that helped me enjoy a successful career in management positions. I here share some early experiences that stayed with me, that contributed to my desire to write this book, and that I hope prove useful to you:

When I first entered the workforce as a teenager to earn some spending money, my thoughts were only on how many hours I needed to work and how much I would be paid. Management was not on my mind. My job was a gas station attendant, working 9 am to 6 pm during the summer months. My boss was Mr. Dudley.

Although I didn't realize it at the time, I learned a lot from him. He explained my responsibilities, what he expected from me, and when a new task surfaced he ensured that someone demonstrated what to do — and then he left me to do the work, learning as I went. And I made mistakes, likely the mistakes he anticipated. I caused gasoline to spill onto cars, missed lubricating some grease fittings, left a steering wheel covered with grease to the customer's dismay, caused a battery to explode due to not charging it correctly, and more. Each mistake resulted in a brief discussion with Mr. Dudley, sharing his concern and showing me again the right way. He never yelled or cursed, and I never made the same mistake twice. I confess, it was only in gathering notes for this book that I revisited those months. There's a lesson there: good management goes unnoticed because, in the process, we're treated as we expect/hope to be treated. I'll revisit this later in the book.

My next experience with management came in the U.S. Air Force, where I reported to a five-stripe sergeant. He was friendly, treated me (a one-striper) with respect, and wrote a superlative performance review for me that resulted in a promotion to two stripes. Of course I was delighted, but I was confused because I saw more experienced persons receiving lower performance reviews.

All I had done was do exactly what he assigned to me. Was my work superior? Or was my review a reflection of his experience with poor performance of prior subordinates? What he had taught me I would later understand — that doing the job assigned, doing it right, staying with it until done, and seeking feedback when needed, were traits that would always help me (or anyone) stand out.

When I asked about my performance review, I learned something that would serve me well many times in the future: he explained that my performance review wasn't based on how the job might be done by an individual with higher rank and more experience; my performance review was based on my performance, considering my lack of extensive experience and my being new in that field.

That sense of fairness; that sense of evaluating a person, not against persons in higher rank or positions, but against the person's knowledge and experience in an entry position, gave me the insight that helped me always address performance and salary increases in a way that was equitable, and never left me feeling I was showing favor.

The experience later in my enlistment term with another sergeant was quite different. He abdicated explaining my responsibilities, leaving that to the outgoing individual who previously did the job, and rarely stopped to see how I was doing the work, or whether I had questions. After a month or so, he called me into a private room to yell at me for not doing whatever it was he had expected, and that he had never explained. That was the first time I realized that being called a manager does not make one an *effective* manager.

The final experience I'll share was one of my more frustrating ones. In that position I had learned to talk to my manager about the work and in what areas to demonstrate my abilities and opportunities to excel. I received many compliments on my job performance that year, yet my annual performance review put me as *good,* where the category choices were *poor, good, excellent,* or *superior.* I questioned my manager on why I wasn't rated as *excellent* or, more desirably, *superior.*

His response was that it wasn't my turn yet. Another person was being groomed for an above-average pay increase and promotion and I would be given a more upbeat review the following year. Being afraid to give me a fair review was what immediately sent me on a job search.

There were many more managers in my career, and I still had much to learn on the full scope of management, but these four were part of my foundation. My hope is that you will enjoy this book and find it useful.

One more thing: The book title. I do not endorse perfectionism and am not a perfectionist. The Perfect Manager, in practice, makes mistakes. Mistakes keep us human and being human is part of what makes for good managers. I just happened to like the title. It's a concept, not a reality.

david shelby kirk
August 2018

"Before everything else, getting ready is the secret of success." –Henry Ford

Management: What is it?

Before moving into the topics, let's first understand the word *management*, at least as I see it. Knowing the vocabulary is always a good start.

Is Perfect Management possible? Obviously not (but it makes for a nice book title). Management is an imperfect art dealing with other people's roles and activities, but I used that title for the book to emphasize the importance of setting the bar high in pursuit of this important profession. Being promoted to manager doesn't make you one; it just changes your title and maybe entitles you to a new business card — and gives you bragging rights to your family. Beyond that, it's all up to you. In many professions (such as doctor, lawyer, plumber, electrician, teacher, mechanic, engineer), there are certifications to confirm the individual's competence in the role, but in others (such as politician, manager), the title stands alone. You can stumble forward (as do many), imitating your peers, or you can take the role seriously and study to be effective. My hope is that reading this book serves you well. Let's start with information on the meaning of management.

The term *management* has always been a problem. That is, we use the word, yet generally have no clue on what it really means. Is it leadership? Not necessarily. Is it good fiscal control? No, but that helps. Is it the ability to meet target dates? I don't think so; that is certainly desirable, but can sometimes have negative consequences. Projects that meet target dates, but deliver mediocre results and demoralize the affected employees are legion. Are my definitions common? No. These opinions would be strongly challenged by some companies because those are the traits they seek.

The downside of focusing on a single measurement is that each can be negative. For example, if staying within budget is primary, quality can suffer and target dates may be missed. If meeting a target date is primary, the work may be over budget and employee morale can suffer due to unplanned overtime. For management to be effective, the employee aspect must always be considered. What I refer to as *Perfect*

Management is multi–faceted, but one must also be able to speak to upper management on real trade-offs to their proposals to change dates, deliverables or funding. But I get ahead of myself...

In considering the definition of management, let's first consider the oft–told story of the blind men attempting to describe an elephant, with each man touching just one part of the elephant. One touches the tail, another the body, another the trunk and one, the tusk. From this, each drew a conclusion that was only partly true. And so it is with defining management. It is very situational to where you are and your role there.

Consider these definitions:

- "The act or art of managing: the conducting or supervising of something." – Merriam-Webster.com

- "Management is the art of getting things done through people." – Mary Parker Follett

- "Management is a multi–purpose organ that manages business and manages managers and manages workers and work." – Peter Drucker

- "Management is, above all, a practice where art, science, and craft meet." – Henry Mintzberg

- "Good management consists in showing average people how to do the work of superior people." – John Rockefeller

Does that help? As you see, even from experts there are several definitions: all true, yet all different. The term *management* obviously must apply to a wide variety of functions, ranging from the role of a corporate CEO to that of a construction foreman. Identifying who is (and who is not) a manager can be solved by looking for a few key features of the work.

Features of management

There are some key features that apply to all management activities. If they don't apply to what you do, then possibly your role is other than true management. Whatever you do as a manager, keep these features in mind to ensure your success:

- Management is always **situational**. That's right; a manager's role is not applying just one technique or skill. What works with one situation may fail in another. A manager needs to be sensitive to the many components involved, whether they relate to people, funding, equipment or the workplace.

- Management is always **results oriented**. Managers aren't usually involved in the day-to-day work. They're an extra cost that is intended to improve or maintain work goals. If what you're doing isn't so focused, then you are likely doing the wrong thing.

- Management always involves **work to be done by others**. A challenge to persons recently promoted to management is to keep doing the tasks they did prior to becoming a manager. That's the sure road to failure, as that isn't why you were promoted. Also, don't confuse being a manager with being a staff assistant. If your work consists of management-type tasks, but you do it for upper management, then you're a staff assistant; if your work is to provide direction for subordinates, then you're a manager.

- Management always includes **authority to influence rewards to others**. This is key. If you lack authority to recommend or deny training for others, or lack the authority and responsibility to set their merit pay increases or promotions, then you're possibly a fore(man/woman) or team leader, but not a manager. Being a manager also carries the responsibility—and obligation—to write and conduct reviews of employee performance.

- Management is always **never ending**. Whereas subordinates may focus on completing specific tasks, the manager must focus on the overall flow of the work and on the work unit's performance against objectives. The manager's tasks are often self defined, requiring the manager to determine what must be done on any given day.

Management Processes

A review of management processes should complete our review of the role of management. Here are the generally accepted five processes:

Planning. This is the core of management, planning for tomorrow. The person successful at planning is the person who looks beyond the obvious and seeks new visions, either to do the current work more effectively, or to create new opportunities or to establish new products from the work performed. Planning is determining the goal and then defining the steps necessary to attain the goal. Once defined, planning is an almost daily activity of reviewing and modifying established plans. Planning focuses on WHAT, WHEN, and HOW.

Organizing. The importance of organizing is often overlooked for its contribution to an effective work environment. Good organizers are able to take a dream and make it a reality. To be successful, one must define the activities of the unit, determine staffing and skill requirements for the work, assign responsibilities accordingly, and also assign authority as needed.

Finally, coordinate how the various components interact for success. A common failure here is to use a textbook approach, assuming there are employees who fit exact skill requirements, instead of assessing what skills are available and organizing to use available skills effectively.

Staffing. Regrettably, this aspect of management is too often ignored or poorly executed, yet is the most visible indicator to separate the great organizations from the good and mediocre ones. The process of staffing includes having quality job descriptions, effective recruitment strategies, appropriate and documented formal performance review policies, cost-effective training strategies, and a fair and easily understood salary and promotion program.

Implicit in effective staffing is knowing what skills you need and how many employees are required. As an aside, you will learn what you need by under-staffing. In so doing, you will discover what shortfalls to correct. With an excess of staff, you may never know your requirements because people will tend to expand work to fill the day. That's human nature.

Directing. This is where "the rubber meets the road." One can plan, organize, and staff with wonderful people and still fail due to lack of direction. The process of directing includes supervising, motivating, demonstrating leadership, and communicating effectively. This is largely a style issue, and what works in one industry or organization may not work in another. For example, supervising one group may require providing detailed instructions on performing the work and on being at work on time, yet supervising another group may be best done by active listening and contributing. Regardless of one's approach, the people need to see you as involved and caring, not distant or inaccessible.

Controlling. Although *Controlling* is the word generally used, *Influencing* may be a more appropriate choice. This management process is another one that oft times is not done or is done poorly. Monitoring and correcting manufacturing costs per item, error rates, attendance, job performance, and target dates are examples of controlling. Whereas the planning process focuses on defining the goal, controlling focuses on execution toward the goal.

This chapter defined the basic ingredients of management. How they are blended into a job will vary widely. Techniques to being successful in one management position, may be inadequate for another. The challenge with the above features and processes is that the degree to which they may apply to a management position varies considerably.

In reading this book, I infer you are a new manager, one desirous or curious about management roles, or one in middle management. Why that distinction? Because managers in senior positions got there through their own style or had absorbed many of the topics in this book through other means. They also may likely hire consultants, attend seminars, or have departments dedicated to doing several of these functions to achieve the results you pursue. As you've gleaned by now, this book's primary focus is on managing at the operational level.

And the next brief chapter gives a conversational view on the core substance to your success. I have found the use of dialogue may open windows of the mind that text alone may miss.

david shelby kirk

"Perfection is not attainable, but if we chase perfection we can catch excellence." –Vince Lombardi

The Perfect Manager

Once upon a time there was a perfect manager. She always achieved desired results; always had employees who were upbeat, talented and hard workers; always stayed within budget; and always contributed new opportunities and solutions. Her employees were empowered to represent her on many subjects, freeing her to focus on the higher level.

As many had done before, a young, aspiring manager approached her with the question, "How do I become a perfect manager?" The perfect manager laughed. The question was all too familiar.

To the young manager she replied, "There are no perfect managers, as management is an art form, being fluid and often situational. The term reflects seeking to do one's best, being sensitive and responsive to the many aspects of management."

Encouraged by her reply, the young manager responded with, "But does that make one a perfectionist?"

"No, no, no. Attempting to be a perfectionist, never having a mistake, just creates stress and annoys the employees, negating any positive impression you intended. You want to do your best, but there will regularly be new challenges—and mistakes—and you will want to seek feedback and help from others.

"Management will be an aspect of your life, but not your whole life. Do your best at work, but always be able to leave it behind to enjoy other aspects of your life at the end of the day. Be sure to keep laughter a regular sound in your workplace."

The young manager reflected on that. Becoming a perfect manager was an attainable and desirable goal. "May I ask one more question? What word of advice might you give as I begin this path?"

The perfect manager smiled. Helping new managers was part of what she enjoyed in her work. "Always remember that, as a manager, you are not better than your subordinates; you just have a different role. You have the responsibility to ensure they receive the information necessary for them to excel. Should they ever sense that you believe you stand apart and above, you are doomed to a mediocre existence.

"Wear the crown of management lightly, as it topples easily. From upper management's perspective, the employees are more important than you. Should push come to shove, you would be the one to go. Consider a sports team or an orchestra: if the team performs poorly, it is the coach who is replaced, not the team; if the orchestra has problems, it is the conductor who leaves, not the musicians."

As the young manager was leaving, the perfect manager offered, "One final word to you: perfect management is a forever learning experience. Let it be a journey, not a milestone."

david shelby kirk

"Before everything else, getting ready is the secret of success." –Henry Ford

Why Are You Here?

Well? Why are you here? Why are you in this management job? Can you answer that? You're a manager, that's great. Congratulations. But what's your job? What are you expected to do? How will you know when you're doing it well? Is your job description written? Before you read another page in this book, you need to answer these questions.

Are you thinking the questions are unnecessary? That the answer is obvious? Those thoughts can be disastrous. People receive the title *manager* for a variety of reasons. Find out yours.

Do NOT go to your manager and ask, "What's my job?" That sends the wrong signal; your manager may start wondering why you were hired or promoted. You don't want that. Instead, I propose you use some open-ended sentences to introduce the topic if your manager doesn't do it. You want your manager to do most of the talking in this particular discussion. Questions such as "What have been the challenges and problems in the past?", or "What expectations do you have for my work unit and how would you prefer that I keep you apprised of activities and results?" would help start the conversation.

And then listen, listen, listen. Paraphrase back occasionally to ensure your manager understands that you grasp what you're hearing. Do not let this be assumed. Be prepared for whatever you hear. Here is an example a colleague of mine experienced:

> "Well, Jessica, I'm glad you asked. We've had problems with accuracy from that department and their last finance report was inundated with errors. Their next financial report is due next Friday and I'm hoping you can get it right. "

Ouch! Not what a new manager wants to hear, right? But it is still good news. She heard of a serious issue and she now knew her first priority. This also gave her the opportunity to identify with the employees and work together to fix the problem. Here is another example I heard from a friend:

"Well, Ralph, I'm glad you asked. People are often late showing up for work here at the office. Your job is to let them know that they need to be on time or be fired. If any of them complain, just send them to me."

Yikes! Ralph's job isn't a manager; he's a bouncer. Words vary for different jobs, but if you detect that you're to be a time-keeper or a baby sitter or a bouncer, you may want to revisit your goal in this job. The good news? Finding out early. A phrase to remember: *Bad news early is good news.*

The Job Description

Many companies have formal job descriptions, generally written in prose that avoids defining the real job. Many may have bulleted lists of the job duties. Here's a sample job description I saw for a sales manager:

1. Develop potential customers
2. Schedule appointments to build relationships with prospects
3. Make sales presentations
4. Close sales and coordinate contracts
5. Advise upper management of results and opportunities

6. Maintain job skills by reading professional publications
7. Participate in local organizations

Desired skills: Develop prospects, meet sales goals, encourage teamwork, and focus on excellence

Is this a job description or a task list? Let's cut to the chase. Most items on the above list are just eye wash; the real job is number 1 (Develop potential customers), and 2 (Close sales). Writing detail duties avoids the importance of having a single paragraph that summaries the purpose of the position. The only necessary skill is "meet sales goals." And whatever is "focus on excellence"? Meeting sales goals is all the individual needs to accomplish. (And there's a gotcha' there: items 6 and 7 could be paraphrased to say, "Increasing your knowledge and skills are your responsibility; the company provides no funding for that.")

My suggestion: write your own and review with your manager. Use terms that are measurable and expansive, avoiding details such as budget or time-lines. Maybe the real job is developing staff to meet sustainable goals or to identify prospects' needs and package existing products to serve those needs.

Your goal here is not to have your manager agree with what you wrote, but to engage in a discussion. That you're writing your understanding of the position sends a strong signal of your commitment to do well, and a wise superior will appreciate the opportunity to discuss the topic. Let's look at a real example, a job I had at a wonderful organization:

The job initially could have been summarized as *Supervise a team of computer programmers*. How's that for dull and lackluster and direction-less. A job description needs to inspire and challenge and visualize the work. Here is a subset of what I wrote and reviewed with my management:

> *Work with departments to develop and manage plans and projects to ensure their business computing needs are appropriately met within a time frame that meets identified priorities. Manage a team of computer specialists to achieve these goals and also review and recommend appropriate technical platforms for optimal execution for the business needs.*

Compared with *Supervise a team of computer programmers*, this shows ownership of the role of the job. Supervising is but one of the tasks of the job, and was never the job itself. With this done, I was free to develop a list of responsibilities with verbs such as

Develop, Ensure, Maintain, Analyze, Monitor, Report, etc.

Bottom line: Some of the above may prove unrealistic in your situation. Do what you can, but do understand the importance of the discussion with your manager. This is always a learning experience and priceless.

The REAL Job

Okay. What you achieved in this chapter is significant, a cornerstone for your time in this position. With the job description addressed, you now have something in writing. This will be a component of any formal performance reviews, so having that in writing has a future payoff for both you and the organization. Now, let's focus on the real job. Yes, the real job is different from the job as documented. That's because the work you will need to do, the skills you really need, are rarely in the job description.

The job description gives you the map, but it is the skills you acquire, the tasks you define and execute, and the documentation and measurements you produce that elevate you to success. Those are the focus of this book and we'll address some of that in the next chapter.

A tip: Management positions generally require more paperwork than you wish, and it's easy to become content in sitting at your desk, producing reports and charts and memos and policies and what-all. Some managers are always at their desks. Avoid that comfort zone; the work for which you were hired is always elsewhere.

Bad News Early is Good News

"One of the most sincere forms of respect is actually listening to what another has to say." –Bryant H. McGill

Open Door Policy

Okay, you're a manager, you've discussed or reviewed or rewritten the job description so that both you and your manager share a common focus. Congratulations. What you've accomplished is almost as rare as seeing pink unicorns. As you move into your work environment, one of your early thoughts might be that hackneyed phrase, *Open Door Policy*. Many new managers feel they need to communicate that to staff on day one to assure them that they are good listeners. DON'T DO IT. Such a policy can become a crutch that implies openness, when it may not be so. Let's listen in:

"Excuse me. Are you busy?" The young manager had stopped by the Perfect Manager's office to talk.

"Oh, do come in," she replied. "My focus today is on the annual merit budget. This is one of the most important tools a manager has, so I want to understand the company's direction for this year. What can I do for you?"

"Well, I noticed your office door was open, so I was hoping you might have a few minutes to talk. Is this what is called an open door policy?"

The perfect manager was startled at the question. "No, I don't use that phrase. Having face-to-face contact with employees is one of the more important roles of a manager, but an open door policy can be interpreted in different ways, usually that the manager is busy, but tolerates occasional interruptions. People don't like to interrupt their manager unless it is very important. So, I leave the door open for walk-ins, but I don't advertise any policy."

"But, but... how do employees talk to you then?" To the young manager, it seemed a contradiction: wanting employee feedback, but not advertising an open door policy.

Being a patient manager, the perfect manager realized the perceived contradiction. "Look, I want you to be successful, so sit down and I'll briefly explain my technique for engaging employees.

"It is really simple; instead of relying on employees seeking me out, I go to them. Each day, at random times, I wander through the work area to listen to conversations, learn new issues, occasionally stop at subordinates' work areas to see how they're doing, offer my assistance, and share topics. Maybe a target date is slipping, or reports from other areas are late, or they may have a suggestion on the work flow. Or maybe the conversation strays to family issues, sports or the weather or whatever.

"Such conversations, although they may seem unnecessary and irrelevant to the work, keep me abreast of each person's work environment, challenges, successes, and personal opinions. These conversations also demand that I know what is happening within the work group. I would lose credibility if I were to ask one of my team, 'What are you working on?' I should know that already."

The young manager found this interesting, a reversal of going to the manager. "Okay, that sounds really good, but don't they resent your stopping by every day? I would think they would feel you're interrupting them or spying on them."

The perfect manager laughed at the thought. "Oh, no. I don't stop at each person's work area daily, just on occasion and never when they're obviously deep in thought or involved in another conversation. I agree, interruptions should be minimal. My approach is to attempt some personal contact at least weekly with experienced staff members and maybe a couple of times a week with new employees or those who have taken on new responsibilities.

"Their success is my success and I work to ensure that message comes across. Each person is vital to the organization and should feel I'm always on their side. And from these discussions I am always highly aware of successes and trouble spots. A side benefit is that, by knowing of issues early, the employee and I can adjust the work to manage issues—and also to plan celebrations."

Following a brief pause, the perfect manager commented, "The other benefit is that, by going to the employees, they know they have my full attention, whereas when they occasionally stop by my office they know I'm pausing work on whatever I was doing when they entered. Giving full attention and active listening are the ingredients of productive discussions."

"I'm trying to summarize that concept, ma'am," said the young manager. "What words might simplify what you explained?"

"Just write *Manage by Walking Around*. It is an old concept, and a highly successful one. Keeping your office door open is still very important, as issues surface routinely. But managing by walking around will serve you, and your team, quite well. Another shorter summation would be *Be There*. Just by being there, you and your team will solve or prevent many problems and also discover new opportunities."

"May I ask one more question? You mentioned celebrations..." Confusion was evident on the young manager's face.

The perfect manager viewed her watch. "Not today, I'm afraid. That merit budget is waiting for me. Possibly we can discuss that at a later date. I hope this discussion today was helpful for you. Before leaving, would you mind summarizing what I've shared? "

Beginning to see the perfect manager's intent, the young manager exclaimed, "That's one of your techniques, isn't it? Giving advice and then confirming that the other person understood. That prevents common misunderstandings, doesn't it? Paraphrase. Say it back to confirm the message. I'm writing that down now, so I don't forget it.

"To your question, ma'am, I can see that managing by walking around is a core skill to team success. There is much that I need to learn, but being involved with the people will ensure that I'm aware of issues. Thank you for your time today."

She smiled. The young manager had begun showing potential, making her time with the young manager well spent. Learning the concepts of planning, organizing, influencing, and control were vital skills to master, but understanding people is number one for all managers.

Manage by Walking Around

Be There

david shelby kirk

"Be a yardstick of quality. Some people aren't used to an environment where excellence is expected." –Steve Job

The Mission Statement

Yes, this chapter is on that much maligned phrase: *mission statements*. No, don't skip to the next chapter; this is important to your success. Do this right and it will pay dividends for years, not just for you, but for your team as well. Mission statements have earned a well–deserved poor reputation for such as the following example:

> *We are committed to proactively embrace high–quality services to allow us to endeavor to synergistically optimize marketing challenges while promoting personal employee growth opportunities in multiple venues.*

Have you read mission statements such as the above? A string of rambling words of nonsense that leave you wondering what the sentence means? Imagine the poor employees who are striving to be supportive of this mission statement. Such mission statements are so prolific that there are many websites poking fun at mission statements that don't connect. Curious? Click on your favorite internet search engine and enter "mission statement generator" or "silly mission statements" or a similar search and you will locate enough web pages to give you smiles for hours.

Do I need one?

Good question. Yes, a mission statement documents

1) the role of your work unit,
2) who its customers are, and
3) what value your unit adds to the organization.

People may work for years or decades at a company and not know this, other than their specific job assignment. Having a mission statement that is clear and concise helps all in your work unit, as well as your customers, have a better grasp of the importance of your unit's role.

For example, let's assume your work unit provides help desk services to customers. An employee of the group might define her/his role as "I answer the phone to deal with complaints." That's true, but that is just one aspect of the job and doesn't address the issue of why the unit exists.

The Company Mission

Does your company have one? Does it make sense to you? Can you read it and see where your work unit fits in and supports that mission? Assuming that the company's mission statement is highly respected throughout the company, consider a conversion with your supervisor on how that individual sees your unit. That's your first step to writing a meaningful mission statement. However, if your company's mission statement doesn't exist, or is a collection of meaningless words, then a discussion with your supervisor may not be a good idea. Know your corporate culture. But you should still do a mission statement for your areas of responsibility; it will pay you back manyfold.

Building Your Mission Statement

Okay, let's start. I already mentioned discussing (or not) with your supervisor, depending on your view of corporate culture. But you do need to discuss with your customers for their assessment and with your team members. With customers, I suggest one–on–one discussions where you can probe for positive (and negative) feedback. With your team, I encourage at least two meetings: one to explain your vision of a mission statement, and one or more to gather thoughts and suggestions for the statement. A by-product of working with your team is that they will help keep the statement from becoming meaningless fluff. Let's listen in:

The young manager was struggling with the idea of creating a mission statement. Seeking advice, he stopped by the Perfect Manager's office, hoping that she might have some time to discuss this. Stepping into the doorway, he quietly intoned, "Excuse me, would you have a few minutes available to address a concern of mine? I've been struggling with doing a mission statement and I don't know where to start."

"Well, you've picked an important topic, for sure," our Perfect Manager responded. "Yes, I can spare a few minutes and I appreciate that you asked of my availability. Time is our scarcest resource. So, you're struggling with doing a mission statement. That's always a tough task, but always worth the time. Tell me what you've done so far in this."

"Not much", the young manager conceded. "As you know, I manage a customer support desk, responding to customer questions and problems. I held a team meeting, but all they came up with for our mission was that we answer questions. That's all we do. How do I create a mission statement from just that? A statement such as *Our mission is to respond promptly to customer inquiries* doesn't seem to hit the mark."

The Perfect Manager paused. "I see your challenge. That's a good start, in that it has a quality component, but what you just described are the tasks you do, not your mission. Identifying your task/role is just the first step. You also need to identify your customers. Who are they?"

Puzzled at what seemed an obvious question, the young manager stammered, "Our customers? I don't understand. Our customers are the people who buy our product. I'm confused."

"That's my point," the Perfect Manager sighed. "Those are just your external customers. Don't you periodically do statistical studies on problems and prepare reports to upper management, especially our marketing team? And doesn't your team make occasional suggestions to improve the product or to simplify interactions with our customers?

"You're still focusing on just the more visible task," she continued. "You need to include awareness of your customers and to also demonstrate why your team exists—the value you add to the organization. One way is to visualize the organization as if your team's role did not exist." The Perfect Manager sat quietly while the young manager digested the information.

Slowly, the young manager began to smile. "You're right", he exclaimed. "We do so much more. My team is part of the marketing component, servicing customer needs and providing feedback on quality and features. We don't just attempt to manage customer complaints; we are the face of the company to our customers and the feedback element to the company. Our service is vital to company success. Although a small element, what we do is seen at many levels. We answer questions, but that's just our task. What we're doing is building customer loyalty."

"I'm impressed with your growing insight," the Perfect Manager volunteered. "Now, can you use that new insight to frame a mission statement?"

"Yes, I can envision it and may need to tweak it a bit with our team," the young manager exclaimed. "How's this for a first cut: *Our mission is to improve quality and expand customer loyalty by providing a superior consumer experience.*"

The Perfect Manager smiled. "Congratulations. Well done. I encourage you to revisit that in a year, as your new insight will grow and you may discover new opportunities for your team and other company departments may envision additional services for you to consider. For example, instead of just responding to customer inquiries, you may wish to consider an outreach program of surveys or follow-ups. When considering customer service, you may find the possibilities are endless, and all discovered by creating a mission statement. Again, well done."

The young manager had much to contemplate, but left the Perfect Manager's office with a new confidence, and all because he now had a mission statement.

david shelby kirk

"Management is doing things right; leadership is doing the right things" – Peter F. Drucker

It's The People, Stupid

Without people, there can be no employees. And without employees, there can be no managers. And without leadership. the good employees will leave. That is the ultimate measure of management performance: keeping the good employees. Surveys have shown that one of the major reasons employees seek new jobs is because their managers ignore employee contributions, scrimp on acknowledging employee successes, and/or lack vision.

In one job of mine, I was a project manager running a large project and also coordinating the work of other project managers. The budgets for the projects totaled in the millions of dollars. Yet, if I needed a pencil, I had to approach the lead secretary who would walk with me to a locked closet 50 feet down the hall and hand me ONE pencil. All for a pencil. The message from management was clear: employees were not trusted and would even steal office supplies (even though the mission statement proudly acclaimed quality employees). I soon found other employment, as did others.

I have known colleagues with impressive MBA degrees, yet who were ineffective in achieving results when working with others. It's the people, isn't it? Regardless of how brilliant we may be, or how creative and innovative are our ideas, if others are not inclusive to the direction, we will fail.

The operative word is *inclusive*. Being polite, always smiling, sharing jokes, or advertising an open door policy are not actions that cause employees to feel part of the work unit. Employees will believe you care when they see that in your actions, not in your words. So, forget the flowery speech and decide your direction.

Managers and Leaders

In management, you can be a manager or you can be a leader. We have a glut of managers, so my recommendation is to strive for leadership. The difference? Leaders stand out from the crowd.

Managers emphasize control of the work; leaders build relationships so the employees can manage the work. Managers focus on time sheets, quotas, arriving on time, not interrupting others, getting through this one day—all being issues that have some merit, but that are shortsighted in dealing with today's knowledge worker. That tactic may have been adequate at a time when efficiency of manual labor was paramount and job opportunities were few, but not today. Employees accepted the environment as being better than having no job—but the world has changed; that tactic produces either poor quality, low morale, high employee turnover, or all three.

Compared to the manager's approach above, leaders will work with the employee skills available, restructure the work to capitalize on those skills, build awareness of expectations, and always be questioning and seeking better ways.

Managers focus on costs; leaders look at opportunities. Managers are regularly known to say the following:

- "We can't do that because it costs too much."
- "You can't have a pay increase because it isn't in the budget."
- "To meet the target date, let's work nights and weekends."
- "That's not how we do things here."

- "We don't tolerate mistakes here."

On the above, leaders are known to say:
- "That's a good idea. If we can prove the benefits, I'll propose to management for more funds."
- "I've been observing your contributions and you'll see a bonus in your paycheck." *(*Translation: a leader is always looking for excellence and is prepared to acknowledge, even before the employee mentions it. The reward might be a new title, a new office or desk, a different assignment, or other options. It does not need to be financial.)
- "We'll never meet the target date without compromising quality. I'll schedule a meeting with management to consider options." (Translation: A leader takes pressure off the employees and shoulders the unpleasant task alone of confronting the sponsor.)
- "We've never done it that way, but I'm interested. Let's review with the others to see how that approach will fit."
- "Mistakes will happen. We just need to learn from them."

Notice the common thread of all leader statements: they are focused on the employees, the people. They demonstrate listening, caring, considering, and respecting. This concern for people and disdain for boundaries distinguishes the leaders. Those example sentences above are idealistic, yet demonstrate the importance of always striving for excellence.

Does that mean that leaders don't need to be aware of costs and timeliness? No, not at all. The difference is one of priority and direction. Managers focus on "running a tight ship", whereas leaders are looking to what opportunities exist and always have a focus on the employees. You can keep within budget and meet upper management's goals and still fail as a leader if you are viewed as separate from your employees.

The Manager Path

Okay, does all that sound too "blue sky" to you? That's understandable. You might want to ask yourself why you think that. My guess is that your thoughts may reflect the corporate culture in which you are involved. Do you see leaders rewarded or silenced? Companies shout that they want leaders and innovative ideas, but that's often just words. Many just want people who stay in line, sing the corporate song, avoid controversy, and do what they're told; employees with leadership potential are quickly eliminated. Many such companies are successful (although they could be better), and you can still carve a path to personal success, but carefully. You encountered this challenge in the earlier chapter,

"Why Are You Here?", so your feelings in this chapter may come as no surprise.

The Leader Path

Unfortunately, when we think of *leadership*, we are prone to think of great people, such as George Washington and others who were daring, brave, brilliant, and outspoken (and often tall). But leaders can also be any height, introverts, have limited formal education, and possess limited experience. What they have is a demonstrable and visible caring for the success of the work unit and well-being of the employees, not just themselves. They stand for what they believe is right.

"Speak clearly, if you speak at all; carve every word before you let it fall." –Oliver Wendell Holmes

Management Speak

Management Speak is a seductive speech pattern; if you're around people who speak it, there is a tendency to also speak it to show how smart, literate and aware you are. A benefit of using management speak is it frees you from needing to find more appropriate words to express yourself. And it happens without realizing it. I well remember when, as a child, I was exposed to a group of friends who used foul language. In only a matter of weeks, my speaking vocabulary was sprinkled with "four–letter words", several of which I didn't even understand. The same can happen with management speak. If you're not careful, you'll be using sentences such as this next example in no time at all:

Going forward, let's synergize resources to action the paradigm shift of customer challenges

when the real message was simply

Let's focus on new customer problems

Are you hooked already? Do you infiltrate your sentences with phrases such as *work smarter, not harder, paradigm shift, big picture, strategize, get outside the box,* and more? If so, you already have the disease, but there's hope. The cure? STOP DOING IT. Why, you ask? Because employees *detest* this management tactic of using fancy words and phrases to make issues overblown and vague. And employees are known to use their free time to laugh and imitate your management speak. Employees may still respect you, but they'll keep their distance. Speak plainly, always. Be specific, always. Tell the truth, always.

Examples

Below are some examples to avoid. And you can always get a grin by entering "management speak" or "management speak generator" into a search engine to see even more examples, many of them humorous, and all emphasizing the importance of avoiding the pitfalls of management speak.

Work smarter, not harder – Offensive, a quick sound-bite with no substance.

Plan forward (and *Going forward*) – Redundant. Forward is implicit in planning.

Paradigm shift – A fundamental change, such as the shift from buying in malls to buying online. Rarely applies.

Team and *Team leader* – See chapter, "Did You Say, 'Team?'"

Pre-plan – Impossible. Oxymoron. Planning is planning

Low-hanging fruit – Cliché – Interpreted as making changes before a thorough assessment of issues. Also indicates an unwillingness to tackle the bigger challenges

From the get-go – Cliché

Get ducks in a row – Cliché

Granularity – Indicates reference to multiple levels of detail. and is not a replacement for *detail*

Stakeholders – Vague. Be specific

10,000 foot view – Employees need detail. From 10,000 feet, you can't see the potholes or the rust.

Incentivise – Changing nouns to verbs can turn off employees.

Leverage – Try using *use* instead.

In a perfect world – Translation: "I admit there is a right way, but let's do it my way, instead." Often used to trivialize an employee's suggestion.

View the big picture – Can be considered offensive. Used when the employee's role hasn't been explained well.

Strategize – Another noun-to-verb example. Plan?

Quality team – Implies quality is an add-on, not systemic.

Helicopter – also, *Run up the flagpole, Send a trial balloon.* Example: Helicopter the idea and see where it lands.

Synergy – Use carefully and sparingly. Explain the result.

Think Outside the box - Cliché. People do not become creative because someone asked them to. And will you support and champion ideas that are outside tradition?

Drill down - Cliché. Avoid. Investigate? Assess?

Action - We need to action the project issues. - Noun-to-verb. Avoid.

Get the ball rolling - Begin? Start?

Take this offline - Talk privately?

Take it to the next level - Cliché

Touch base - Cliché

No-brainer - Cliché

Short chapter, huh? Yeah, the subject was a real no-brainer, but I wanted to action your leveraging the plan forward from the get-go to get the ball rolling to incentivize your taking this management topic to the next level. Did I just say that? Horrors.

Summary

To be effective, use words and phrases and sentences that are clear. Clichés and management speak reduce the effectiveness of your message. Simple words are always preferred to big or infrequently-heard words. The goal is communication, not obfuscation.

"Great things in business are never done by one person. They're done by a team of people." –Steve Jobs

Did You Say, "Team"?

Do you refer to the employees in your unit as a *team*? Are they? It is the kind of statement that makes people feel good, but only when it is true. It is the kind of statement that managers quote to inspire their employees. It is the message unfortunately given when the manager needs the employees to work overtime or forego vacations or otherwise subordinate themselves to a corporate objective and postpone their personal objectives.

The word *team* is too often used when management feels the need to inspire employees. But employees aren't so easily fooled. Use the term *team*, but always after you're sure the term fits. Otherwise, it is just a four-letter word. Let's listen in to the Perfect Manager:

One of the young managers stopped by the Perfect Manager's office and discovered her staring out her window, likely contemplating a complex issue. Hoping not to interrupt her reverie, the young manager commented, " Good morning. I was passing by and noticed how well your team works together. Have they always done so?"

At the compliment, the Perfect Manager's eyes sparkled as she turned to reply. "Thank you. No, they didn't always work that well; the answer is in the wording of your question: team."

That puzzled the young manager. "Team? Isn't that just another word for an employee group? I hear managers using that term frequently, usually when attempting to inspire their group."

Shaking her head, the Perfect Manager sighed. "Yes, unfortunately. Managers like to associate their work groups with sports teams, but just referring to them as a team sidesteps how teams are formed."

"Okay, I'm confused," the young manager confessed.

"Let's consider football teams," responded the Perfect Manager, hoping to show an example. "Each player has a specific role and trains for that role, but also works with the other team members to confirm that each individual role meshes effectively with the others' roles. When it doesn't, they modify their roles as needed. This isn't done just once, but regularly. Further, they all know the plan, the strategy. No player is ever wondering what the play is to be, whether it is a running play or a passing play, or where the ball-carrier will attempt to run. Some roles have more visibility to fans than others, but all are vital to success. All of them.

"It is by such interplay that individuals will see themselves as being part of a team. No one needs to tell them. No fancy speeches are needed. When people see themselves as being in a team, you have a team. Until then, all you have is a group of employees. Does that explanation help?" The Perfect Manager inquired.

No longer confused, the young manager posed the question, "Thank you. Yes, I can see how a sports team must practice together to create that team bond, but how do people in business do that? My group does billing and we don't have time to practice creating an invoice or handling remittances and credit issues and other aspects of our work."

"You don't have time?" the Perfect Manager sharply responded. "That's one of the biggest roles in your job. It may not be in your job description, but employees who see themselves as a team are what fosters excellent performance as opposed to just good performance. That's your job, so you need to find the time."

The young manager was taken aback, having never heard the Perfect Manager speak so strongly. "I'm puzzled; we have a full work load and there's no time to give training classes. What am I missing?" The young manager was clearly troubled.

Patiently, the Perfect Manager spoke, "Look, you're making the forming of a team into a one-time training session. That doesn't work because team building and reinforcing is an ongoing experience. Consider the football team analogy: the person I didn't mention was the coach, whose job is not to teach the game fundamentals of football. The players know the game and that's why they were hired, just as your employees were hired: because they have the skills or potential. The coach is there to help them play better, to learn where their skills fit, and to lead them to their own success. Yes, their own success. When a team wins, the players know it was their performance on the field that won. They did it, not the coach.

"Remember an earlier discussion where I mentioned the tactic of managing by walking around? Watch a coach in action. Although there are times the coach addresses the players as a group, most of the time the coach is watching players in action and giving personal feedback. It's the combination of both techniques: group involvement and individual focus. And it takes time; you do not build a team in one day or one week. They will know when they are. You will see it in the respect shown among them. No one on a team is unnecessary." The Perfect Manager paused to let the young manager digest her words.

The young manager felt encouraged. "Thank you for your time. I hadn't realized the importance of the word *team,* or that team–building was an ongoing process. Just being part of a work group does not make one part of a team. I have work to do and I'm looking forward to it."

"I'm so pleased that you're seeing the value of building a team attitude," the perfect manager responded. "In doing so, you will find yourself not alone when faced with unforeseen challenges, and you may also see more ownership being assumed by employees. Teams are a win for everyone."

david shelby kirk

"We hire people who want to make the best things in the world." – Steve Jobs

Hiring – An Art Form

Managers have few opportunities to change their work environment. Most of the time, managers find their time is spent just keeping things moving properly. That's where the bulk of the work is, and that's what upper management looks to you to achieve, so don't take it lightly. Still, you need to influence the process and the outcome. One of your best opportunities is in the hiring process, because that's where you bring new ideas, new skills, and new enthusiasm into the environment. This is also where others will see what people you think will do well. In the hiring process, you are judging what persons to hire, and upper management is watching to see your preferences and, over time, how well the new person succeeds.

For example, let's stay with our football analogy of the prior chapter. When a new coach is hired, people acknowledge that the coach is working with players during the first season who were selected by the predecessor . The new coach shows his/her mark on the second and later seasons when selecting new players. And it's generally in the third and fourth seasons when the coach is judged on performance, because that is when people assume the players are ones the coach selected and coached.

Your hiring history may not be that visible, but never assume that it isn't known. Hiring good people then, is not just good for the company; it's also good for you. The person who is good at selecting the right people is invaluable.

Before continuing, let's review your role. The intent in the earlier chapter, "Why Are You Here?", was to help you confirm whatever your responsibilities and authorities are in your position. Did your role in hiring get discussed then? It isn't uncommon in some companies for the immediate supervisor to have little or no input to hiring. You can make that type of world successful for you, but that denies you the important experience achieved in the hiring process of evaluating and selecting persons to be part of your world. You need to have "skin in the game" to learn from this process—and to share some accountability for the new employee's success.

Okay, enough on the company politics. Let's focus on the hiring process. In fact, let's start well before that. A phrase to always keep in mind:

Work Expands to Fill the Time Available

And there's another thought to keep in mind:

How much work does the work unit have?

And also this one:

Are there new opportunities to explore?

Those three thoughts should always be concerns when contemplating hiring new people. Specifically, just because everyone seems busy doesn't mean there is sufficient work to justify the number of employees. You might have too many (and that may open a door to new opportunities), or you may have too few (which could identify the importance of restructuring the work or exploring opportunities to improve performance, e.g., hire more employees, share with other departments, outsource specific tasks).

Two important issues

1. Just because you may have too many employees should never automatically justify a layoff. Laying off experienced people is sometimes necessary, but experienced employees are scarce—and they know the work, know your company, and are known in other departments. Priority one should be an attempt to locate work in other departments or, better yet, propose some new service to upper management that might salvage their expertise.

2. Just because you may have what you perceive as too few employees should never automatically justify hiring more. The benefit of *not* hiring immediately is that this gives you the opportunity to discover where the shortfall exists, if at all. Does the shortfall occur all the time, or just at certain times, such as end of month or quarterly? Is there a work flow issue that needs revisiting? Whatever you discover, you will need to feel strongly that there is need for more employees and what skills they need and how they would fit into the organization.

Did an employee quit or retire?

When an employee leaves, there is a tendency to immediately seek a replacement. Resist that. This is a rare, and possibly welcome, opportunity to rethink what you need. Did a supervisor leave? That may be an opportunity to reorganize. What skills were lost? Are they still needed? Look at all the work, from the bottom level on up. There are always opportunities to improve a work unit. Typically, employees will assume or request that the open position be filled with the same responsibilities. Fight that; your role is to have the vision. This is also an opportunity to *not* fill the position, at least not now.

My suggestion: wait. See how the work is affected, if at all. Hiring a direct replacement should be a last resort. Why? Because hiring a direct replacement can be viewed as not having a vision and not seeking new opportunities. You may still decide to do that, but you will sleep better, knowing you investigated other options. As a manager, such opportunities don't come often.

Seeking Candidates

Filling a position quickly can seem an immediate priority, especially after you've done some investigation and made a decision on what the new person will be doing. Go slowly. It's easy to hire someone and next to impossible in many companies to get rid of them. My recommendations:

1. Write the job advertisement. This may not be the formal definition, but should reflect what you need, not what your ideal may be. That is, if you want a person with a graduate degree, be sure the job actually *needs* that to succeed. An advanced degree may help the chosen individual learn the job more quickly, and a person with more education than other applicants may offer more potential, but be careful in making that a requirement, or establishing any requirement that restricts applicants without strong evidence on the need. More than once in my life I have been hired when I had none of the defined requirements for the job, yet excelled anyway. I recall one former supervisor of mine stating, "You were not what we asked for, but just what we needed."

Job descriptions (covered in chapter, "What Do Your Measure") that are highly detailed on minutiae generally reflect how a trained employee of several months or years might perform, not what an applicant should be able to do. Focus on the essence of the job, not the mechanics. Your goal in writing the job advertisement is to attract applicants, not to discourage them. For example, I once needed a person to serve as a help desk coordinator. One of the applicants was a waitress from a diner. At first, her experience may have seemed inappropriate, but the skills of dealing with many people, managing priorities, and keeping track of different needs were all there. Had the job description been too rigid, she may not have applied.

2. Evaluate your current staff carefully, as one or more may desire filling the open position. Can they do the job as you want it done? That is, hiring a new person is one of few opportunities in your career to employ the people whom you believe can help you achieve your vision for the work unit. Moving current employees to new opportunities has its own payoffs, but don't lose focus on bringing new blood and ideas into the group.

3. Go carefully in considering friends of employees. It's human nature to recommend one's friends when a job position is open, but your goal is not to hire people, but to position your work unit for success. You cannot afford to have people thinking that your role is to find jobs for people, or to have new employees seeing their friend as the one employing them instead of you.

4. Diversify. If your work unit does not represent people of different color and gender, you are missing opportunities. If your advertising isn't receiving applications that indicate diversity, it may be that you are not advertising in places where they will know of the job.

5. Seek other opinions. If your company has an HR (Human Resources) department, there may already be a formal process of how interviews are conducted. If not, consider establishing a small group of employees from other work units to assist in reviewing applicants, leaving the decision to you. If done, I encourage meeting with them prior to the interviews to review your goals and requirements for the open position.

6. Don't fight HR, but do work with them. Their focus is on equal opportunity and fairness, not necessarily on hiring the best person. That's your job. My experience is that this can be a good working relationship. BUT, always remember that HR works for the company, not for you. HR is *not* your "friend", despite whatever you may hear. HR is a resource, for sure, but they will assist you only when your wants match what the company wants.

7. Prepare for the interview. There are many excellent books on the topic, so I recommend you read a few, rather than a few sentences from me. This is the main event where you must not only identify the person you want, but also provide the excitement to cause applicants to want the job. Three guidelines:

a. Ask no questions that don't relate to job performance.

b. Do ask open questions instead of yes/no questions.

c. Let the applicants do most of the talking.

The First Day

Almost every employer screws this up, the first day on the job, yet this is really the day that sets the vision for the new employee. What happens on this day is what the employee will long remember, what the new employee will share with family and friends at the end of the day. You want that to be a feeling of enthusiasm and high expectations. The solution to this is simple:

BE THERE!

So, what does that mean? It means making sure you're available that first morning, that when the new employee shows up that you are there to greet her/him, make introductions, spend some time discussing the work, your vision, why you hired the person, what some of the challenges are and what some of the opportunities are. And also be sure to advise where, and from whom, help is available. This needs to be a priority above whatever else might be placing a demand on your time.

This isn't a 2-3 minute task. I'm recommending a minimum of 30 minutes, and an hour or more would be even better. The more senior or professional the position, the more time is needed to set a proper tone. You're laying a foundation with the new person, so don't rush. My suggested steps are here:

1. Tell the current staff a little (not a lot) about the new hire the day before the new person starts. This eases tension and avoids surprises and increases the possibility that one or more employees will approach and welcome the new person.

2. If the company requires a trip to HR or other work units for new employees for forms, id tags or whatever, then you are the one to be the escort. Having one's new supervisor take time for these mundane processes reduces stress and builds a platform of loyalty and commitment, a sense that you and the company really care.

3. If the employee's work entails working with persons in other work units, take the time to introduce them. If personal visits aren't possible, then find other ways, such as phone calls or email to make the introductions. New employees get up to speed more quickly if supervisors open doors for them early on. And that's your obligation to them.

4. Have work for the new person. Obvious, isn't it? Yet I've seen too many new employees show up and be given a few manuals to read because there was nothing to do on the first day. New employees have a strong desire to make an impact and such an experience will not be soon forgotten.

Why does this happen? Usually because there is the general assumption that the current employees aren't getting all the work done and the new person will immediately know what to do and step in—but usually the current work is being done, either because you're not understaffed, or because the employees have been working harder or smarter to finish the work. A downside of not having work for the new person is that the current employees may inadvertently assign the new person where you had not intended.

Prevent this by planning early where the new person can contribute during the first few days of becoming oriented to the work. This is also an excellent opportunity to do something new without taking existing employees from their work. Be creative here. The payback is enormous.

Summary

Okay, does doing all this ensure you get the right person? No. But by going through all the steps you will learn a lot about hiring, and by the fifth time you do it, you will have devised your own strategy to success. Doing things "my way" is never the goal; the goal here is giving you ideas for your own success.

Yes, you will sometimes hire someone who "doesn't fit" with the job. We'll talk about that in a later chapter. Just accept that mistakes happen and it's not a failure on either side. You may discover that you asked for the wrong skills and maybe the applicant found the work didn't fit the applicant's expectations. Stuff happens and we grow from the experience.

"Success is not the key to happiness. Happiness is the key to success. If you love what you are doing, you will be successful." – Albert Schweitzer

It's Not a Pyramid

Let's focus briefly on you. You're reading this book to learn some tips or ideas on being a successful manager and I felt a chapter, possibly brief, may be worth some contemplation. Inspiring people to find the meaning of life isn't my strength, so I won't attempt that. However, what I will do is provide some basic information on what lies ahead in the world of management so you can explore that jungle and discover your own findings.

My other reason for including this chapter is that, depending on where you are within the company hierarchy, your position will demand emphasis on some skills more than others.

First, although the term *pyramid* is frequently used to describe the ladder of advancement, it just doesn't fit. Pyramids rise from the base gradually and consistently to the top. Company hierarchies aren't even close. For my example, let's assume there are just three basic levels in a company. Some companies have more, but those are minor variations.

1. Level 1: The workers
2. Level 2: The middle managers
3. Level 3: The senior executives

Level 1

To form a visual picture of a company hierarchy, let's build a more realistic structure than a pyramid. First, visualize level 1 as a large pizza box. This level forms the base of any organization: the workers. These people can be identified because they have specific skills that they execute every day and have no, or few, supervisory responsibilities. This level includes analysts, technicians, administrative staff, secretaries, programmers, custodians, engineers, electricians, machinists, truck drivers and all other positions that actually "do the work" of a company.

I wrote this book with the assumption that you are managing, or will soon manage, a work unit at this level, for it is at this level that the full range of management skills are most productively used.

People at this level are generally content/happy with their role, respected for their skills and recognize that working together is necessary for success. These people also are generally more successful that those in level 2 and 3 at balancing their life with work, family, and personal interests. Predictably, salaries and responsibilities can vary greatly at level 1 depending on the company itself.

Level 2

Now place a match box in the center of the pizza box. We'll refer to this as middle management. Notice the significantly reduced content size. I wrote this book with the assumption that you are here, or soon will be. (I didn't place you in level 3 because people there either already have the skills to be successful managers, or think they have. I will have more to say on that in the chapter titled, "Further Reading.")

We generally think of people at level 2 as having been competent performers at level 1 with the additional skill of leadership that influenced their promotion to level 2, but that would be only a textbook view. In reality, people arrive at level 2 from different paths. For some, it's the traditional path, but some arrive at level 2 directly from college with only management potential — no experience, and others arrive as transfers from other functional areas to exert their management skills as needed.

Regardless, they all have a competitive nature and a desire to influence the work as done by others. Translation: you're in competition with them to some degree, whether that's your intent or not. Be open and cooperative with these peers, but be careful in assuming that everyone is a team player. Some aren't. And the competition to be promoted upward can be fierce because, above this level, there are few positions available.

If you are the manager of level 2 subordinates, your challenges and opportunities will generally be quite different from dealing with level 1 subordinates. This happens because they aren't new to the work world and have developed a variety of management–related job skills and are aware of the unspoken infrastructure within the work unit. A positive aspect is that they have their own management experiences, both successes and mistakes, to bring to the unit. Your challenge is to build on this talent by coaching them in leadership and in building coalitions among groups. They already know how to do the work; they grow from expanding their own management and team skills.

Level 3

For the highest level, place a thimble in the center of the matchbox for our senior executives. Space is tight; there isn't room for many and competition to be here, and to stay here, can be tougher than lower positions — and the risk of losing one's position is far higher.

Your success here is dependent on your ability to lead, to inspire, and to be a visionary — and to never forget the fundamentals of the business. Your challenge is in expanding your view beyond the company, seeing the community, the economy, and new opportunities. Your work hours will often exceed 60 hours a week and your phone will always be with you. There are benefits, but there is also a price.

You're on your own at this level. Your success will depend on how effectively you manage yourself in an expanded world.

Summary

Is there a bias in this chapter? Did some personal experiences sneak in? Does a cow moo? Of course. My point here is that a company is not one big tent of happy workers with similar motivations and expectations. Instead, a company consists of multiple camps, each with its own view of the world. Stay focused, find where you want to be, and remember that success is not measured by income, but by personal satisfaction. Remember the structure:

Thimble
Match box
Pizza box

It's no pyramid.

"There is nothing so useless as doing efficiently that which should not be done at all."
— Peter F. Drucker

"Anything not worth doing is worth not doing well."
— Robert Fulghum

Focus Focus Focus

In writing this chapter, I think of the civil rights song, "Keep Your Eyes on the Prize", as the emphasis is the same: to succeed, one must not be distracted from one's goal. Many a promising career has faltered because the individuals became distracted. This chapter is just a refresher on the importance of remaining focused.

Branch Rickey, the famous American sports executive, once said

"I don't care if I was a ditch–digger at a dollar a day, I'd want to do my job better than the fellow next to me. I'd want to be the best at whatever I do."

Is that you? My guess is that it is. Otherwise, you wouldn't be reading this book for some ideas and tips on becoming a better manager. But being a manager is not the same as digging a ditch. The ditch–digger, working diligently at his/her task, is not bothered by interruptions, but can exert full focus on the shovel and the dirt. You're not so lucky.

If we can assume that you have a good working environment and are managing it appropriately, you will have a powerful sense of achievement and purpose. But managers always have unwritten components and situations in their jobs and are sometimes distracted from their mission. Such distractions can kill a promising career, so I added this chapter to ensure the topic is on the table. The following paragraphs are intended as examples only.

- **Don't excel at trivia.** Doesn't make sense, does it? We're taught from childhood to always do our best. Your challenge is in deciding how you want to be perceived by others, the operative words in the paragraph title being *excel* and *trivia*. Assignments taken need to be properly done, but excelling may not always be your best move. And whether or not the assignment is trivia can only be decided after assessing the impact it may have on your career.

Upper management frequently are in need of people to do peripheral tasks, whether chairing the annual holiday party, coordinating a tour of the office for some school children, attending a luncheon for a charity, taking minutes for some manager meetings, etc.

When asked to do tasks that are far outside your responsibilities, it may be a high compliment to you as a rising star, but before you celebrate, consider whether senior people were passed over in giving you the assignment. If so, could it be that you are, indeed, a star? Or is it possibly "busywork" that others eschew? Do the assignment, but remember it's not your primary function, and it may either open new windows of opportunity if that's your perception, or, if upper management sees you as an outstanding meeting secretary or chair of the holiday party, your promotion opportunities may become permanently narrowed.

- **Don't focus on winning arguments to the detriment of solving a problem.** You've heard the phrase, *Win the battle, but lose the war.* As a manager, you're likely competitive and like to win. Just remember what it is you want to win.

- **Don't focus on getting credit instead of achieving a goal.** This is hard. You work hard on a project and some people perceive the work was done by another. Instead of raising your flag at the end of an assignment to proclaim your achievement, routinely keep the appropriate persons apprised of your involvement, including tasks, milestones and issues. And if you share credit with all participants publicly, you will have strong support from them on future initiatives. Everyone wins.

- **Don't compete with staff on who is best.** Let's face it. As the manager, there's a good chance that there are portions of the work that you can do better than your subordinates. But that's not your job. Your job is to coach them so that they can do their best, not compete with you.

One of the biggest challenges new managers face is in transitioning from their non-management role to their new one. This happens, because they're good at their old job and still learning their new one. It's normal, but the sooner one stops it, the sooner one's staff can focus on their jobs.

- **Don't say you're quitting until you actually do.** Okay, I included this little tidbit, just in case things aren't working out as you wished. Never threaten to quit your position unless you're walking out the door for good. Never even hint that you can get a better job somewhere else. The tactic may serve you in the short-term, but you will be forever viewed as dispensable, disloyal and untrustworthy. If you plan to leave, avoid any temptation to seek revenge on the way out. Focus on where you're going, never on where you've been.

- **Don't play favorites.** It's that simple; just don't do it. You likely have one or two employees who excel and volunteer regularly to assist, but it may be that others are just slower in responding. Ensure a level playing field by approaching different individuals periodically when having special assignments to do.

Doing this prevents a perception of there being favorites, spreads the opportunities fairly, and helps you assess strengths of your team. I will have more to say on this issue in the chapter titled, "The Merit Budget."

- **Don't avoid problems.** That this is one of the major failings in many organizations should come as no surprise. It's not uncommon within a work unit for there to be an employee who routinely avoids some of the work, causing managers to bypass them when needing something important or quickly accomplished.

This is no secret, as all the employees are aware of those who are not contributing. In a prior position I held where I terminated a non-performing employee, I was approached the following morning by a remaining employee who commented, "I didn't think a manager would ever get rid of that individual. Thank you." Avoiding this problem will cast you as weak and untrustworthy, a manager who doesn't support the team. I will have more to say on this in the chapter titled, "Time to Go."

Summary

To summarize, distraction is what destroys managers. In the prior chapter titled, "Open Door Policy", I stressed the importance to BE THERE when listening to staff members, as they quickly ascertain when you're looking, but not listening. This chapter repeats that emphasis, but throughout your role as manager.

When in search of excellence, there is no other way.

Stay

Focused

"Telling an introvert to go to a party is like telling a saint to go to Hell." — Criss Jami

Parties and Other Stuff

Let's get one thought out of the way: to many people, the phrase *office party* is a four–letter word. Ignore that at your peril. The words *party* and *office* will always be a problem, mostly because they're in conflict with each other.

Okay, now that we've covered that, let's talk about parties. Since they're in conflict with work, you will always have issues; it's just part of that territory once you enter management. The biggest challenge is one of personalities: extroverts and introverts. Outside of work, this is never a problem: extroverts and introverts find their own way, select their own friends, and celebrate life in groups of their choice. But when people are assembled in an organization to do work for pay, attempting to create a festive environment that will please them is a road filled with potholes.

Some people believe that extroverts like people and introverts don't. But that's not true. Extroverts are energized in the company of others, while introverts are energized by ideas. For example, in a work group attempting to solve a problem, introverts will be active participants, but at a social gathering of small talk, the extroverts will be the ones most heard.

From my experience, you will most likely see a preponderance of extroverts in a marketing, sales or customer service work group, and most likely to see a preponderance of introverts in technical fields. Generally, though, roughly **half the population** are introverts. People find that difficult to believe, but I believe that is because extroverts make their views more public.

I recall an event where a department manager of computer programmers (who was an extrovert) held a holiday luncheon for the employees and had food catered to a large conference room where he envisioned the employees would eat and talk and enjoy each other's company. Instead, the employees came to the room, filled their plates, and then returned to their cubicles where they shared the time with close associates. The conference room was left empty, and the manager was angry that no one was *celebrating*. It was what I call a "bad party": the employees were content, but the manager didn't understand what had happened—and was doomed to repeat the error the following year.

At another job where there were approximately 40 employees in the department, a group of three extroverts proposed a holiday party of drinking and dancing. The department consisted solely of technical positions, yet the manager gave the okay because the group indicated "everyone loves a party", and when the other employees were asked their opinion at a staff meeting, no one spoke. Very few went to the party. Another "bad party": the handful of extroverts and their invited guests got to dance, but they were mostly alone. Whatever the manager's objective for the party, it wasn't met.

The challenge you face as a manager is that it will be the extroverts who will be routinely proposing having a party, and they can be quite vocal in their pursuit and their sometimes perception that "everyone loves a party." Following their lead can cause you to have what I call bad parties. Yes, there are good parties and there are bad ones, and most fall into the bad category.

Good Parties
Did your team spend weeks or months on a major project, possibly working many extra hours per weeks

without overtime pay? Whatever the details, justification for a good party demands that all participants feel strongly involved in the reason for the celebration, and that the reason goes well beyond daily activities.

My suggestion: use the word *celebration*, not *party*. Why? Because the word *party* invokes visions and memories of unprofessional activities, which you do not want, not ever. After all, you're a professional organization. Parties are known to have liquor, dancing, and what may be inappropriate socializing. You cannot afford any of that.

Good parties have several attributes:

- Good parties have a PURPOSE. Your team is a professional work group and everything they do should address a purpose of yours, the manager. There is always a cost, so be sure you know WHY you're having the party.

- The justification is obvious, such as a long project with much non–paid extra work hours.

- The event is held during work hours. Why? Having a gathering after hours is telling your employees that they must give of their personal time. If what you have is an event to celebrate, doing the celebration during work hours keeps the event a reflection of the work achievement and you guarantee 100% participation. When done after hours or off site, the participation drops, and the objective you had intended for the celebration is compromised.

- Family members are not invited. Because the event is work-related. It's that simple.

Bad Parties

After defining good parties, bad parties are "everything else." Okay, by now you're likely thinking that I'm a socially-challenged, nerdy, uptight, tedious, misanthropic, hermetic dinosaur whose underwear is too tight. After all, "everyone loves a party", right? Well, no, they don't. Still convinced I'm wrong? Consider these reasons for bad parties:

- **The party is to help the employees bond.** Bond? Employees bond to your needs by working together. Your best approach to resolve this issue is to restructure the work flow so that the employees understand the importance of the others' contributions—and that may generate ideas to improve the work flow. Throwing a celebration/party for people who don't work closely together causes each clique to form in separate groups, not come together in the expected bonding experience.

- **The party is to have some fun.** *Fun* is a vague term, indicating you may not yet have a reason. Parties always have a cost. The question is always, "Was it worth it?"

- **I want the employees to like me.** There's a lot of truth in that, not just for you, but also for me. We want to be liked, especially if we're the manager who sometimes has to make hard decisions. True, there are employees who will tell you what a great person you are and how super the party was and will ask excitedly about the prospects of the next party for the group. Remember: you need respect, but business is not a popularity contest. Never was, and never will be in professional offices.

- **It's Christmas.** No, that's not a good justification. One of the most disliked of all parties is the "Christmas (or Holiday) Party." Attempting to blend the local holiday spirit into the work environment will always be a challenge. The most successful Christmas Party I've witnessed was where the manager held an annual celebration on a day near Christmas with a catered buffet from 11 am to 3 pm, held all phone calls and email, and gave employees the rest of the day off. Attendance was 100%, people talked and laughed, and then left at their discretion.

Exceptions

There is a special category of "office party" that defies my "good" and "bad" definitions: the annual (Christmas?) dress–up party given by upper management that is always at night, usually a Saturday, and often with liquor and dancing. Yes, it violates everything I said, but this dinosaur continues on. I call it an exception because it's going to happen with no consideration on the benefits or purpose. These aren't parties or celebrations; they're pure theater. These tend to be well–attended, giving the impression of being liked, but consider the attendees:

- Managers attend because it's their duty; it's "part of the job" to show up for such events.
- Employees attend because they're fearful that not attending will put a bad light on their loyalty.
- Senior managers attend because it's an opportunity to let the employees see them.

My guess is that such parties have a high cost, generally more than $100 per attendee. My recommendation: Give each employee the money and a half–day off and you'll have happier employees.

Other Options

That's right, there are options to all of this. Your true goal is showing employees the results of their contributions and expressing your appreciation. That's the real initiative to celebrate. BUT, I respect that you may just want to lighten up the workplace now and then. There are many ways to do that. Some samples here that might get your creative juices flowing:

- Ugly sweatshirt Fridays
- Bagels at all staff meetings
- Set up a break room with coffee, snacks and a game or two and chairs
- Hold meetings outdoors periodically

Remote Workers

If some of the employees work at home and interact electronically with other employees, then it becomes its own priority to occasionally create opportunities for them to meet face–to–face with peers—and that works best if the purpose is to review a work–related topic, not just have coffee and bagels. Be sure to do it. Remote employees should always be invited to all group events. Even if they don't attend, they need to know they're invited and welcome.

Summary

Okay, I rambled a lot on this because I've seen so many failures in attempting to keep employees happy. If you focus on their success, the celebrations will take care of themselves.

Celebrate

Don't
"Party"

"What's measured improves." – Peter F. Drucker

What Do You Measure?

Quick answer: You measure performance.

Next question: How do you do that?

Quick answer: By having meaningful job descriptions.

Next question: How do I create those?

Glad you asked. Good job descriptions are rare, and I've found it can take several years and iterations before you get it right, usually after reviewing an employee's performance and finding the individual's strengths or weaknesses are not addressed in the job description, indicating a need for a revisit. Writing meaningful job descriptions is hard work, but has a strong payoff in helping employees expand their roles and understand their own performance. Even the simplest job should require at least 30 minutes to write a description, and positions at high levels may take many hours, plus reviews with others for concurrence.

Doing this right will save days and months in the future. One of the big benefits also is that such a job description will yield a higher percentage of desirable candidates applying, as they will have a good grasp of what the job requires. Let's get started.

The Job Description

The Job Title

First, give the job a working title. You may change it later, but defining it now can help you flesh out the details. The first words a potential applicant sees is the title. If it seems vague or inappropriate, they will skip it. For example, is you're writing a job description for a clerical position, the job title of "Clerk" may seem proper to you, but it provides almost no information. Is it simple filing, running errands, serving as a receptionist, updating financial records online, or what? Or, consider an analyst position. Business analyst? Systems analyst? Financial analyst? When defining a job title, some thought on the required skills is mandatory to ensure you receive desired applications to be submitted. .

The Duties

Next, do the hard part: define what the person in the position is to do. Try to keep it to a paragraph, not too long. I suggest writing with a focus on deliverables to emphasize that the work is results–oriented. If the position does multiple functions, show the percentage differences, where possible. That situation is most prevalent in smaller organizations or departments where a person may have multiple duties. The description should also specify if the position requires interaction with other departments or the public, If that is a significant aspect, consider making that a separate paragraph.

The Skills

Now that you've defined the job title and duties and interactions, this next step is more clear cut: Define the skills. Be specific where appropriate. For example, I've seen job descriptions stating "Familiar with office software." What does that mean? Ability to type? If the person must be proficient in specific software or features, then state it. However, it's easy to overstate skill requirements. There is a tendency to define skills as we wish the perfect candidate to possess, but is that your minimum skill requirement? If you're open to a person growing in skill knowledge, maybe the job can be performed by a person, in this example, who is familiar with using spreadsheets, not necessarily proficient.

My recommendation is to define the skills, but avoid the degree of performance, letting that be addressed in performance reviews (in next chapter) or during the interview process. Be sure to list all the primary skills, as in the next chapter, we will be developing metrics for each skill.

Another trap to avoid is writing requirements that are based on the person who most recently had the position. That individual may have contributed skills more expansive than the job requires, leaving you with a gap after departure.

However, there is a potential upside to that. If a prior employee substantially expanded the role, then I suggest a review of what was being achieved, versus what the job description indicated. Otherwise, you may find yourself with an out-of-date job description which serves no one.

The Attributes

Following skills, define the personality attributes you value for that specific job description. Those might be communications, leadership, teamwork, flexibility, adapting to periodic changes in the workplace, and others. Again, as with skills, we will be developing metrics for key attributes in the next chapter, so be sure to define the attributes that are key to success in the position.

TIP: There is a tendency for employers to dump every conceivable personality attribute into every job description. After all, don't we all want people who are excellent communicators, have leadership potential, work well in teams, are highly flexible, take ownership of issues, seek opportunities for growth, are polite and friendly, bathe daily, brush their teeth, and share our values? Yes, but dumping all that into job descriptions reduces them to meaningless verbiage. Stick to just defining those you can measure.

The Salary Range

Finally, place the job in a salary range. Showing a low and high lets applicants develop an expanded perception of the position and allows you more flexibility in negotiations because the applicant sees the growth potential, even if eventually offered the job within the lower part of the scale. Ideally, the salary range will be one of the corporate job salary ranges. That protects both you and your employees.

A Job Family

Okay, we now have a job description. Is this part of a family, such as junior business analyst, business analyst, senior business analyst? If you do, then you do yourself and the company a favor by copying the description you wrote and expanding or contracting the definitions of skills, attributes, interactions and duties to create a family of job descriptions.

There should be many shared words and sentences, but a clear difference in the expanded independence of higher positions and more dependence of lower positions. Give each its own salary range and you've defined a career path that can support your vision of your work unit as its role expands in the future.

The downside of a job family? Yes, there's almost always a downside. In this case, the downside is that employees may infer they will be promoted to the higher position as their salary increases — but in reality, that should only happen if the work demands it. That is why it is imperative to have documented the interactions, duties, skills and attributes to demonstrate that the work has different demands and expectations at the higher levels in the job family.

This chapter covered nothing radical, did it? Yet most job descriptions are either a thin list of fundamental tasks of no use, or documents so dense that deciphering the real job is impossible. If you're in a large organization, your HR department will likely want to review your work and modify to fit a corporate template. Here, diplomacy is your friend: fight, but cooperate. Your desire to create better descriptions is your strength.

david shelby kirk

"Strive for continuous improvement, instead of perfection." – Kim Collins

Performance Reviews

Before starting this chapter, think back on some of your own performance reviews. More than likely, one or more were disappointing, upsetting, frustrating, and discouraging—or were so full of flattery that you left with no awareness of what you did, or should continue doing.

Managers have a history of avoiding such reviews because discussing performance details makes them uncomfortable. This causes many of them to either blast the employee with every mistake to shore up their own stature, or to shower the employee with praise to avoid any meaningful conversation on specifics. Why are they uncomfortable? A lack of information to prepare adequately for the review is a common explanation. Another reason is possibly a lack of understanding on the importance of the review, causing the review to either be done quickly — or often not at all.

You needn't suffer as those managers do. In fact, my hope is you will look forward to performance reviews with your employees, as that is one of the best ways to bond, define common ground, and build a solid base for growth and career direction. This is also your best bet to communicate to the employee that you do care and have a desire for their success. Let's start at the beginning of successful performance reviews.

First, performance reviews need to be positive and constructive. If employees dread the thought of having a performance review, then you are already the loser. And where I mentioned it should be positive, I did not mean it to be flattering or avoiding shortcomings, but to show support, direction, encouragement, and confirmation of achievements.

For success, place yourself in the role of coach, looking to help each person grow and participate in the process. That means you should not *ever* spring a performance review on an individual without both of you having had advance preparation.

So, how do we do that? The performance review process consists of three basic steps:

1. The manager prepares for the initial meeting with employee, reviewing business goals and past employee performance to establish a base line for discussion.
2. The manager and employee meet to revise and jointly agree to annual objectives for the employee.
3. The manager and employee meet periodically throughout the year to review and adjust objectives as needed.

The first two steps require the most work, as they set the baseline for the year. Note that merit pay and promotion are not part of the performance review process. Let's follow the Perfect Manager and see her approach to establishing that baseline:

"Ma'am? Do you have a moment for me?" Our perennial young manager stepped hesitantly into the Perfect Manager's office, clearly showing frustration. "I have to do performance reviews and I'm scared of how employees might react."

Looking up from her desk, the Perfect Manager allowed herself a smile; performance reviews are a one-on-one exercise and can be daunting to new managers. "Good morning. Yes, that's a tough topic, but I'm busy at the moment. How about stopping by in an hour for coffee and we can discuss? Does that work for you?"

Feeling a sense of relief, our young manager happily agreed.

Meeting later in the day, the young manager was anxious for help, blurting out, "HR told me that I needed to do performance reviews of my employees, but I don't know what to say to my team. Some are doing okay, some are doing very well, and a few might do better, but I don't want to sound like a parent, and I'm not sure they would understand where I see issues. They seem to work well together and I want the discussions to be helpful, but—"

"Enough," the Perfect Manager gently interrupted. "I can see you're upset, and understandably so. Employees are people and each of us deserves honest and useful feedback, yet many would–be performance reviews miss the mark. Consider, for example, that some companies use simple check lists for performance reviews, with statements such as *Completes work assignments* or *identifies and corrects errors* and other drivel, accompanied by check boxes for *poor*, *good*, or *exceeds*. I consider those atrocious, hideous, ghastly, disgusting, and embarrassing. You may have to use such a form to comply with corporate policy, but people deserve better feedback on their contributions than just a few check boxes marked on a template; they deserve to see objectives and their performance toward those objectives in writing.

"That check box approach works well in assessing performance of small children, using topics such as *Doesn't run with scissors* or *Shares toys with others* because that is for review with a third party, a parent, and not for constructive dialogue with the child. With adults, such templates fail because 1) the template wording is owned by the employer, and 2) it's a "once and done" process.

"Making a performance review effective requires that both sides have a scorecard in which they both participated. So, use corporate forms if you must, but I encourage using other forms to ensure you and the employee make this a productive process and not something reminiscent of receiving a grammar school report card."

The young manager was puzzled. "A scorecard? What in the world is that? I thought that term was just used in sports."

The Perfect Manager smiled. "Yes, that's right; I use the term here to reflect that, for a performance review to be constructive, the employee should already know the agenda, the expectations, the employee's prior contributions, and the manager's expectations. So, I call it a *scorecard*, but others may refer to it as an simple assessment worksheet. Let me explain.

"Remember my comment on being a coach? A coach doesn't give performance feedback only after a game, but early in the season and periodically throughout the season, helping the athlete increase and sustain performance over time. That gives the athlete the needed information to work on issues, using sessions with the coach for continual feedback. That applies also here. The employee deserves early knowledge of expectations and objectives."

The young manager's eyes lit up with excitement on this new revelation. "So, the performance review session comes last, and the first meeting is just to define expectations and objectives? That makes so much sense, yet I hadn't thought of that. That gives the employee the information, so that there are no surprises when the performance review is done. Wow!"

"Exactly!" the Perfect Manager cautioned, "but there's work in doing that. As the manager, you need to have reviewed the skills and attributes from the job description earlier, defined the performance level for each skill and attribute, and also defined your perception on the employee's ranking in each.

"The simple format I use is a spreadsheet with a row for each skill and attribute for a job specification, but never more than seven or eight per skill category, and all categories should be broad to allow employee empowerment. Then, I add several ranking columns for the skills to show the standard, plus similar columns to rate the employee. This gives the employee a simple view of my understanding of the job requirements and also of how the employee is fitting into the job. This format becomes an easy tool to encourage discussion."

Hastily taking notes, the young manager commented, "That sounds rather simple. Would you have a sample spreadsheet I might use for a template?"

"Well, it may not be an exact fit for your needs, but I'll be glad to provide you with one," The Perfect Manager happily responded. (NOTE to reader: See www.pm-worksheets.davidskirk.org for the template.)

Clearly puzzled again, the young manager probed, "But... but this process seems incomplete. What does the employee do with the document? Something seems to be missing. "

"Remember," the Perfect Manager asserted. "That is just the scorecard, showing where the employee's knowledge and performance fits into the job description. But that's mostly to help the employee grasp the depth of the position and the growth opportunities; as a tool to assess performance it fails due to lack of any information specific to the employee's performance. For that, we need a document that reflects joint agreement on direction."

"So, the scorecard isn't enough?" the young manager gasped. "There's something else needed? And it must be a joint agreement? How do I do that? This is starting to look like work."

Laughing, the Perfect Manager cautioned, "Yes, it's work, but important work, possibly one of the most important tasks a manager can perform. Time spent helping employees focus on their success pays off every day. Securing joint agreement is rather straightforward: you need a common agenda to discuss and then document. I'll review the steps briefly.

"First, you should identify the aspects of the work that apply to the specific employee. Not everything, just some major components. For example, maybe there's a key monthly report to develop, or a new product to document, or a training program to administer, or whatever can be defined more explicitly than just *Meet all job expectations* or other such tripe.

"Put these on a performance planning worksheet for the individual prior to the initial review; there shouldn't be more than five or six key objectives. And, these are just your suggestions; in the session it is imperative that the employee take ownership of the objectives. I will share a sample performance planning worksheet with you, but the format isn't as important as having one that works for you and your team. (NOTE to reader: this worksheet is available for your use by downloading from www.pm-worksheets.davidskirk.org.)

"Next, you conduct the initial review. With a copy of the scorecard, the employee and you can first discuss your assessment of the employee's knowledge and experience to date. In doing that, be open to changing your assessment, as the employee may introduce information on past accomplishments or skills that you forgot or overlooked. Otherwise, the employee may justifiably feel it's a one–way discussion—and then all meaningful conversation ends. And then you're 'toast.' If word spreads that your performance reviews are just management theater, your credibility will be in shreds.

"Although agreement is desirable on this baseline review, it isn't mandatory. Your goal is joint understanding; where you and the employee disagree, be sure that you both understand areas of disagreement before ending that discussion. Once you've established a baseline on the scorecard (and agree to revise as needed), do introduce the performance assessment worksheet that has the objectives you previously identified.

"With the performance assessment worksheet that has your defined objectives for the individual as the discussion tool, encourage dialogue on the employee's view of what you wrote, what the employee thinks are priorities, ideas the employee may offer in any area, and any personal objectives the employee wants to achieve in coming year (such as gaining knowledge in a job skill or formal education).

"And a reminder: this is just the initial session. You want this to be a constructive discussion where you both come to agreement on what will be on the assessment worksheet form for future performance reviews throughout the year. Be sure to schedule a follow-up meeting within a couple of months for review and adjustment. That ensures the form stays a living document. And remember: one of your management techniques is *Managing by Walking Around*. That keeps you in regular contact so you are always familiar with what is happening. Is the process starting to come together for you now?"

"I'm trying to grasp it all," the young manager summed. "If I can summarize what you explained, I first create the scorecard to represent the job description's key components and my current assessment. Next, I prepare the performance assessment worksheet for joint planning for the coming year, and then I have a work session with employee to discuss them both and find agreement on a plan forward. I'm building more confidence; I can do that. But there's more, isn't there?"

"Yes, yes, yes," the Perfect Manager exclaimed. "What we've discussed so far is setting the base line. To me, that's the most important part of performance reviews: setting an agreed-upon direction minimizes any misunderstandings as the coming year progresses. However, what follows are also important: the periodic reviews. "

Periodic Reviews

Let us leave the Perfect Manager for now. She covered the difficult first steps. What remains are the periodic reviews. These should be done informally and with some regularity, the purpose being to have a framework for open discussion on the work and the objectives. For some, these may be weekly, but they need to be done at least quarterly. Otherwise, the entire process becomes just management theater.

These discussions are *not* intended to provide the manager with a platform to rebuke or in any way find fault with the employee. Managers sometimes lose sight of their own goal here, which is to help the employee. Dates may slip, objectives may be missed, and deliverables may be sub-standard. Use that information for education and understanding.

People want to achieve and it is not uncommon to set a performance bar too high when doing initial planning. Accept that as a teachable moment for you both, adjust anticipated results and continue forward. By that sentence, I do not mean to accept mediocre performance. Instead, use this knowledge in your ongoing assessment of employee potential and in adjusting how the performance may compromise objectives for your work unit. Remember the folk song: "Keep Your Eyes on the Prize." The next chapter will help guide you through an equitable pay approach.

PERFORMANCE REVIEW PROCESS:

- Define base line
- Come to agreement
- Do periodic reviews
- Avoid ties to merit pay

david shelby kirk

"It's not about money. It's about the people you have, and how you're led." – Steve Jobs

The Merit Budget

If you want to have an active discussion with your staff, just talk about the merit budget; it's guaranteed to invoke a heated discussion on the amount, the perceived unfairness, and comments about other employees who are paid more than others. Since such discussions can easily fall into negative territory, many managers avoid the discussion, missing a meaningful opportunity for team communication.

However, the above quote from Steve Jobs is right on target: if people enjoy their work and feel part of the vision and the pay is fair, they will stay. Unfortunately, many managers fear reprisals if they mismanage the merit budget, so they give the company's announced percentage to each employee, regardless of performance. Such bungling of one of the most powerful items in a manager's toolbox is a sign of personal weakness and lack of leadership— and employees recognize it quickly.

Don't fall into the trap of giving up. As a manager, one of the most powerful tools you have in growing your team to success is effective use of salaries and merit pay. The operative phrase in my first sentence above is *the pay is fair.* The purpose of a merit budget is to pay each person a fair wage, acknowledging individual performance as the guide.

The Trap of Not Managing the Budget

When a manager announces at a staff meeting the merit pay budget, making a statement such as, "The merit budget for next year is 3%", this causes the employees to infer they will each receive a 3% increase. And, all too often, that is what happens— such a waste of an incredible opportunity to influence staff performance.

The up and coming excellent employees will feel unappreciated, and the employees performing at a lower level will feel comfortable that they will receive an increase, despite their mediocre contribution to the organization. Worse, this reinforces the belief held by some that all employees are entitled to be rewarded equally, regardless of performance.

That approach continues its downward spiral when the manager blames the merit budget when meeting individually with employees to review performance. Although I do not ever recommend marrying performance reviews with merit pay, if employees see that all are treated the same, regardless of performance, you will have reduced both performance and merit pay to theater. The manager doing this is viewed as ineffective, a pawn of the company, and may even offer the apology of "Gee, that's the best I can do. I'm only authorized 3%." Again, don't fall into that trap. Manage the merit budget; don't just be the messenger.

Doing it Right

The problem with managing the merit budget is thinking that is the place to start. Instead, it's the last step in a long walk. The prior two chapters gave you the tools, so it gets easy here. Having done the job descriptions and constructive performance reviews, your work now with defining merit pay allocations (and promotions) becomes straightforward because you have a supportive paper trail and employees who know where they stand. Let's start.

You already have some basic information:
1. The salary ranges for the employee job descriptions. (If such do not exist, you can craft

a rough approximation of what the position is worth at high and low end. Work with HR on this.)
2. The current salary of each employee.
3. Your assessment of employee performance.

With that information, all you have to do (yes, it is that easy), is to map the performance to the salary range. An employee whose salary is near the high end of the salary range should be doing outstanding work to receive any increase at all.

Let's take an example. Assume a job category that goes from a low salary of $30,000 up to $50,000, where the announced merit pay increase is 3%. The following chart demonstrates possible merit percent.

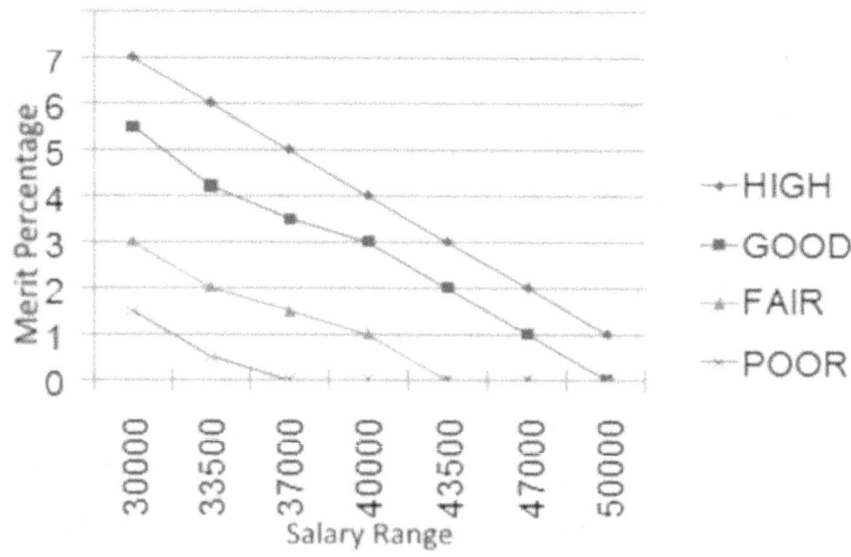

The chart on prior page is only an example to demonstrate the concept and some might consider it harsh, but I built it on the premise that a person doing a "good" job is being appropriately paid at the midpoint of salary which, in this example, is $40,000.

A person performing better than "good" at a lower salary deserves a higher percentage increase and a person whose salary is above the midpoint is already being paid for higher performance. Let me emphasize that: they are ALREADY BEING PAID for doing work above the standard. A person earning $47,000 and only doing "good" is OVERPAID and, although a good employee, should have NO increase in pay. Doing that automatically frees more funds to distribute to those with lower salaries who are performing well. Likewise, a person earning $47,000 and doing high performance is already being paid for the majority of that work and deserves only a small increment, if any at all.

Does that seem unfair? Not really. You have a great performing employee at the high end of the pay scale and your emotional desire is to keep offering that individual as much of a salary increase as possible. That emotion is natural, but that attitude overlooks the performance for pay of the other employees.

The 3% in this example would pay off better if reapportioned among more junior staff. There's another consideration: continuing to pay merit increases to persons at the high end of the salary range whose performance does not reflect it causes the individuals to be in the precarious position of being more subject to a lay-off, should that become necessary.

The real challenge in this situation is to consider whether there is a real promotion opportunity for the high performing individual, a position with bigger responsibilities, not just a fancier title. Doing "make-believe" promotions for the sole purpose of paying a person more will come back to bite you. And other employees see through it. If a real promotion opportunity does not exist, this may be a time to talk to the individual, explaining that the job being performed is appreciated and that their work is valued, but future pay increases will be more from any cost-of-living distributions.

Common Issues For Equitable Merit Pay

1. **Comparing performance of senior personnel with that of junior personnel.** People in lower positions should never be measured to the same standard. If employees are performing high for their job descriptions, their increase percentage should reflect it.

2. **Using the cost–of–living index to rationalize giving equal percentages to all employees.** Your job is not to keep employees level with the cost of living. That's upper management's role in setting the budget itself. Your job is to distribute your allotted amount to reflect employee value for work performed. To reemphasize: that is YOUR JOB, distributing your allotted merit amount to reflect employee value for work performed.

3. **Exempting long–standing employees.** This is common, exempting senior people from the review process, giving them the budgeted amount because of loyalty and time served. This is likely the primary reason that merit budgets are mismanaged. The senior people who are solid, reliable, but still performing on an average scale, need to understand that, as their salary reaches the higher end of the salary range while their job performance remains in the middle of the performance range, they are being overcompensated and their annual increase must be less, with no intended negative message being sent.

4. *Hiring competent people low in range to "save money."* Managers may be encouraged to pay as little as possible for new hires, and when a strong

employee is hired low in range, the manager is likely complemented for the short-term feat.

The real problem surfaces at merit time when the manager must now acknowledge the high performance, yet cannot authorize the pay increase that the employee deserves. High performing employees who sense that their performance is not recognized due to small merit increases may leave for better opportunities. The solution: when hiring, offer a fair amount.

Is There a Tool for This?

There are likely many spreadsheets or other tools to help in reviewing salary distributions, but I developed my own spreadsheet to demonstrate the concept and that may assist you by having a simple tool. See www.pm-worksheets.davidskirk.org for the example worksheet and documentation. I offer it "as-is", but it can be a base to refine to your own needs.

Final comment: Is my style too strong for your company? Do you have a lot of senior employees who are paid much more than newer employees, yet performing at the same level? To me, this is a problem and not one caused by the employees; it is caused by mismanagement. In the final analysis, the decision is yours to make.

From my experience, HR departments are hesitant to support denying merit pay to any employee because many believe that it is also a cost-of-living increase, also known as an "annual increase." Annual increases are fine if the company can afford it, but should be separate from merit pay. The problem HR gives you is in often pretending it is merit pay when, if fact, it is intended as an annual increase. Remember, HR is not your friend, but a colleague with whom to negotiate.

david shelby kirk

"Have no fear of perfection — you'll never reach it." – Salvadore Dali

Your Performance Review

Okay, we've discussed reviews for your staff, but what about you? For your personal growth, you also need feedback and you should want, and even insist, on receiving that feedback. By receiving a review, you may find that a particular result that gave you immense pride was viewed differently by your manager. Such situations are an opportunity for discussion.

Whenever possible, propose to your manager at the beginning of a review period that you want to write your own objectives for the review period and then review periodically for adjustment and agreement. Your process may not mirror what I wrote in the chapter titled, "Performance Reviews", because your manager may have her/his own preferences, and because your objectives may be more open-ended, with stretch objectives to expand your work unit's role and contribution. Also, to achieve a high level of effectiveness, I encourage two reviews: one with your manager and one done by your team. Yes, by your team.

The Official Review

You want to be reviewed on where you're focusing your energy, not on a generic set of topics dreamed up by HR and used by all departments for all jobs. That isn't a criticism of HR; they would likely prefer that each department own this, but few do. WARNING: In writing your own, avoid writing any goals that are meaningless or accomplished by default. All goals should be such that they might not be met. In this situation, including references to target dates and budgets are valid and encouraged.

Where possible, have two categories: a list of goals important to your manager and a list of goals important to increase effectiveness of you and your team. The goals that are important to your manager would be the traditional business-related goals to maintain and/or expand the business; that is your opportunity to document your growth goals for the work unit, goals that set you apart and demonstrate your expanded view of your position. The goals for your team would be specific to increasing their overall effectiveness. Such goals are often not a part of traditional objectives in a company, so you are the one to take that ownership.

Ensure all are within your authority and achievable. For example, a goal of "Attend management training workshop" is dependent on your manager's approval of the workshop's cost and your being away from the workplace for several days. Here are examples of deliverables to increase team effectiveness that are within a manager's control. They may not apply to your profession, but might give you ideas.

- Establish written standards to ensure consistent quality of project deliverables
- Create skill matrices for all team members and a self-assessment worksheet
- Expand team skill set to include support for whatever-is-new-for-you technology

Does the above seem similar to the earlier chapter on performance reviews? It should, but it is also different. In the earlier chapter, my focus was on establishing a standard framework to help your subordinates have a predictable, fair, and understandable process for performance reviews. In this chapter, my focus is on

YOU, revisiting some of the same steps, but from a higher perspective.

The Team Review

What you also need is a performance review done by your subordinates. YES! A review of your performance by your employees. Most managers would rather have a root canal than endure this, and that is the very reason that your success, and the ongoing success of your department, requires that you get that feedback. Despite your worst fears, those people have no desire to insult you or embarrass you or in any way create an uncomfortable relationship with you. But they would like the chance to give feedback, even though doing so may seem more scary to them than to you. So, how do you do that?

First, define what your obligations are to them. Sound easy? Probably not. As managers, we think of what we seek from employees and only rarely, if ever, what they expect from us. The list of your obligations becomes your performance review worksheet for them. Don't attempt this until you've worked with the people for at least six months, preferably longer and definitely AFTER you have done reviews for them. Consider this your management litmus test. If you're hesitant to do it, that is an indication that you're still building a relationship with your team. That's normal, but do it before two years go by.

When done, you may discover that you and they are in good communications, far better than you may have imagined. Should it be done annually? Probably not. It is too exhausting. But every few years? Definitely. Here is an example set of obligations that I once wrote and reviewed with subordinates:

Responsibilities to team:

1. Keeps team informed about departmental procedures, policies and general information.
2. Shares departmental information that may affect our role, the work environment, or our direction/future.
3. Identifies training opportunities and supports employee career initiatives.
4. Ensures all team members are aware of, and working towards, established priorities.
5. Provides constructive feedback on work performance in a timely fashion.
6. Supports team members in dealings with projects and customers and with department management. Consistent and predictable.
7. Lets team members do their jobs; shares the blame and the glory.

Your next step is to review with team in a group environment for clarification and process. Ensure each member has a copy and ask that they meet as a group without you within two weeks (that is, give them time to schedule within their commitments) and, for each topic,

- Vote 1(poor) to 5(very good) by each employee.
- Average the numbers to ensure anonymity.
- Include at least two (but not more than four) statements of constructive feedback, either positive or where improvement by you is suggested.

Encourage them to take at least an hour and to appoint one of them to write up the results.

Finally, when you receive their report, review it in private to internalize what you're reading, but also review it at an upcoming meeting with them. This is an opportunity to acknowledge shortfalls and discuss their suggestions. Don't be surprised if you hear useful feedback. A REMINDER: Do not do this until you have worked with team for at least six months or more, having given them time to know you better. Their feedback will be what you wouldn't get anywhere else.

So, you're likely interested in the feedback I received. Here are some of their constructive comments, exactly as originally written:

⇒ sometimes shares info without the necessary details

⇒ not sure if team input and concerns are being taken back and championed to upper management

⇒ needs to share meeting minutes from manager meetings

⇒ no high–level overviews are available on supported systems, increasing the time for new members

⇒ technical documentation is not current. help us make that happen

⇒ provide more feedback on how we can improve

I was doing some of the above, but clearly I wasn't communicating it well. All of the constructive comments were important, and I ensured they were given proper attention. There were also several positive statements on what I was doing well. Those were appreciated. You want and need that, as those are the tasks you want to continue doing well.

Did I pass? I received an average score of 3.51 (all members votes divided by the number of questions).

The score would have been 4.10 or higher, except I took a hit on question 4 about working toward established priorities. The team decided to give no numeric score for the question and the feedback was "Management needs to clarify the priorities first."

Wow! Great insight and a strong sign of their empowerment. They were right. Within the team I had worked on setting priorities, but they wanted to see the bigger picture, which was *not* being given to them. Without this review, I would never have known their collective view on this vital aspect of how they attached their work to corporate goals.

My word to you: Just do it. Your colleagues may think you're committing suicide—but you know better. We only improve with feedback, whether we play football or manage a team. Seeking that feedback is sometimes difficult because we want only to hear positive/complimentary statements, but it is from the negative/constructive feedback that we change and improve.

"Failure is the key to success; each mistake teaches us something." – Morei Ueshiba

Time to Go

Management books, including this one, extol the virtues of building teams, encouraging growth and innovation, and embracing personal achievement as part and soul of successful organizations. But there's another side we either ignore or hope resolves itself: the unproductive employee. Whose problem is it? The manager's? HR's? The employee's? Identifying what caused the situation is important to confirm, but that is rarely done, because no one wants responsibility here.

However, if the issue isn't about a non–performing employee, but one who has threatened others or may be a danger within the work unit, then go immediately to HR for guidance. There could be legal ramifications and you will need guidance. Other than that, this chapter focuses on the non–performing employee, not a potentially dangerous one.

If you've reached the point where termination of a non–performing employee seems the only remaining path, step gently. This is a failure in one or more ways: a failure to communicate, a failure to hire the right person, a failure to know what skills the work required, a failure to identify new opportunities, a failure to train in the work, and a failure in instill a sense of responsibility.

Yes, it is easy to say that termination is the employee's fault, that the employee was lazy, indifferent, unskilled, too tall, too short, disinterested, unkempt, vulgar, argumentative, fostered dissent, disrupted the work environment, and whatever else you might think of – but you're the manager; you had a part in this.

Termination is costly, and you're the one charged with effective use of assigned resources. There will be loss of overall productivity of the work unit, possibly several months of interviewing and working with HR, acclimating a new employee into the work unit, and dealing with predictable apprehension of remaining employees who may think their jobs are now insecure. And there may be true dollar costs for the termination. This can also be a tragedy for the affected employee and that always deserves serious consideration.

All of that notwithstanding, if termination seems appropriate, it is your duty to proceed. Too many managers, becoming aware of the work required for a proper termination, decide to do nothing. Instead of correcting the problem in the work place, they redirect work to other employees, complain to their peers of having to keep a non-performing employee, and rail against HR for creating roadblocks and requiring "too much paperwork" in the process.

What Went Wrong?

Okay, before doing anything, first do some assessment on the issue. There is a problem and you're part of it.

- Is the employee really a "problem", or is it that your personalities don't mesh easily? Does the employee disagree, argue, or offer criticism on the assigned work? Such assertiveness may be difficult to accept, but this is often a signal that the employee feels capable of bigger assignments and is trying to help you and the team make a bigger contribution. Also, if the employee is popular with your other staff, that is a big signal that you're not seeing the full picture, as employees are usually the first to recognize when other employees aren't doing their share. As the old song goes, "Keep Your Eyes on the Prize." If the work is being done and the individual is accepted by others, then the problem is YOU.

- Had you been anxious to fill an open position and hired the person without a thorough review of the individual's background?

- Did you hire the individual because he/she would accept a low salary, making it appear a "good hire" to upper management?

- Did you meet periodically with HR on this issue? HR reviews such issues from the corporate perspective and can advise you of other considerations. Your first such meeting should never be the one to propose termination. Instead, as soon as you perceive an issue is the time to contact them.

- Most important, have you used the performance review process to give explicit direction, feedback, and support to the individual on multiple occasions so that the employee is aware of the performance shortcomings?

Do You Have Documentation?

Aha! That's the normal downfall. Do you have written documentation, either on paper or email, of every discussion or act of non-performance of the individual? Do recent performance evaluations reflect this non-performance? Did the employee receive a merit pay increase in the past year? Did the employee receive copies of all of these documents at the time they were written? Did you document in detail your several meetings with HR for review and suggestions?

Doing so is VITAL, as HR can advise on legal aspects as well as other considerations in dealing with any employment issue. It is imperative that you show due diligence, not just to document shortfalls, but also to demonstrate that you attempted to help the individual improve performance. Incidentally, if you follow the performance review process diligently, you have ready documentation on all staff members all the time.

The Termination

By now, you just want this stressful situation behind you. Go slowly in these final steps. The individual's self respect must be preserved and there may be legal entanglements. Coordinate with HR to protect you, the company, and the employee.

There is a sadness in this and, doing it once will help you plan to minimize or eliminate this event in the future: better hiring, better training, better introduction to the work unit, and better performance reviews. No one wins in a termination. If there is any benefit here, other than learning the cost of terminating an employee, it is the opportunity to rethink the job. Reread the chapter, "Hiring –An Art Form."

Termination is costly, and you're the one charged with effective use of assigned resources.

david shelby kirk

"The inability to delegate is one of the biggest problems I see with managers at all levels." – Eli Broad

Do You Delegate?

Do you delegate? Most managers will consider the answer to be obvious: "Of course I do" will be the response. But that's not what they do. Instead of delegating, many managers just assign tasks: do this, do that, believing that the act of assigning a task without allowing for discussion, understanding, and capability is the act of delegation.

Worse, managers are also known to abdicate, assigning a task and then avoiding all future involvement, virtually ensuring failure by the subordinate. Another management style is to procrastinate, not assigning the task until it is too late to do properly, again ensuring failure. With a history of these failures, a manager may well respond to the question of delegation with, "Well, I tried, but it never works."

Let's pause here and look at the above from the subordinate's perspective. First, giving terse directives of the "do this, do that" framework is demeaning, sending a strong signal that the subordinate is just a lackey, expected to complete a task and have no involvement in its success. Second, subordinates see assignments where there is too little time to complete successfully as traps against the employee. Those acts plant seeds of distrust among your staff that are difficult to eradicate.

What this adds up to is that managers generally do NOT delegate and do not WANT to delegate. It is important to digest that and probe WHY that situation exists prior to any discussion on HOW to delegate. To assist in this, I've assembled some common reasons used to avoid delegation. And to be sure I communicate the importance of delegating, you must delegate, or you will drown in an excess of work that one manager cannot do alone. It's that simple: delegate or drown.

Delegate

or

Drown

Why Managers Do Not Delegate

These examples may not be complete, but definitely are on the short list of why delegation isn't done.

1. I can do it better myself. A common reason to not delegate is the belief that you can do the task better yourself. So? No one's arguing that. The statement is probably correct—but that is NOT WHY WE GOT THE JOB. We're the managers, not the workers. There are two issues in this:

- Delegating the tasks that got you to where you are will build your team, improve morale, increase overall productivity, and demonstrates to your management that you have growth potential. YES. All of that. Before becoming a manager, you may have been the super spreadsheet guru in the accounting department or the strongest person on the loading dock—but now your job is bigger.

- You need to also identify those tasks that only the manager should do: developing new customers, identifying new opportunities to grow the business, defining where you want your work group focused in coming year, etc.

Activities that shape the direction of your work group need your attention. Keeping the two categories of tasks separate is vital.

This reason to "do it yourself" is embedded in all of us. I recall years ago when I had just been promoted to sergeant in the military, my assigned subordinates were unloading some new office equipment for our group and I jumped onto the truck to help. Not two seconds passed before a seasoned senior sergeant wearing seven stripes yelled out, "Sergeant Kirk, get off that truck NOW!" That was my first (embarrassing) lesson, yet it took many more before I grasped the importance and role of command.

This tendency to do it yourself is also well documented through history. One of the last places where I would expect to see management advice would be in the Bible, but there it is: from the book of Exodus, chapter 18. Moses had just delivered the Israelites from Egypt and had a productivity problem: people were standing in line all day to seek his directions because Moses was making all the decisions himself. And then his father-in-law (Jethro) saw what was happening and approached Moses and gave him this advice:

"The thing that thou doest is not good. Thou wilt surely wear away, both thou, and this people that is with thee: for this thing is too heavy for thee; thou art not able to perform it thyself alone." (King James Version, Exodus 18:17–18)

Jethro then explained the concept of delegating through multiple levels of management to ensure information was readily available throughout the masses. And further on we find the result:

"So Moses hearkened to the voice of his father in law, and did all that he had said. And Moses chose able men out of all Israel, and made them heads over the people, rulers of thousands, rulers of hundreds, rulers of fifties, and rulers of tens. And they judged the people at all seasons: the hard causes they brought unto Moses, but every small matter they judged themselves." (Exodus 18: 24–26)

So, we're not alone in this struggle. Practice, practice, practice will get you over this wall.

2. I'm too busy. Yeah, right. That reasoning for not delegating is circular. Such managers are too busy BECAUSE they're doing it all themselves. Okay, I'll yield one point: doing a task yourself the FIRST time is probably quicker that assigning to someone else and explaining the issues and providing any needed training. That's a given. The time savings (and they're extensive) come into play on the third, fourth, fifth, twentieth and hundredth repetition, and on and on go the savings. And the side benefit of this is that your subordinate now has a bigger view of the organization's contribution to the whole. That is priceless!

3. I won't get credit. Hmmm... To the manager using that as the reason to not delegate, my response would be, "Do you really want the credit for still doing a task you used to do when you were in a lower position?" As a manager, we get credit, not for the task itself, but for having built an organization that gets the work done. Is there a downside? Not really. Other managers with open positions will seek to recruit from your team — but that's a compliment that doesn't go unnoticed by upper management.

Also, by building a strong team, you position yourself to be promoted. What you do *not* want is for upper management to keep you in your current position because you're the only one who can do the job. (TIP: As a sidenote, never ever ever ever ever allow yourself to be the chair of non-productive tasks, such as the holiday party or summer picnic or annual volleyball competition or anything similar. Why? Because if it goes well, you will be STUCK with the assignment forever. I mentioned this in a prior chapter, but it's important. There, you've been warned.)

4. My subordinate might get promoted. This is possibly the worst reason to not delegate: fear that a subordinate's work will shine so brightly that the subordinate might get the promotion which you covet. That fear can eat into your personal life, causing you to challenge the value of your skills and experience, and keep you from using your subordinates' talents and skills appropriately.

As such, you will be viewed as accomplishing less, and will feel emotional pressure to do it yourself, which we have already reviewed. This quickly becomes a downward spiral, as you will find yourself looking for only mediocre employees when hiring. Do not let that happen.

Should you be so honored as to have one or more subordinates who show great potential, then celebrate your good fortune and actively work with them so they learn and assume delegated assignments to show their mettle and to improve your work unit's productivity and visibility—and be sure to give credit for their work. The odds that you will eventually have an outstanding subordinate are high, so take the high road. The benefits? There are several:

1. Yes, your subordinate may rise above you, but as you groomed the individual for the promotion, you will be viewed by upper management as a strong developer of people and your newly-promoted subordinate will always value your contributions. I have personally experienced both sides of this experience and it works exceptionally well.

2. Having a strong subordinate is one of the best ways to position you for promotion. Upper management will see that your organization will continue to thrive, even if you take a new role.

As a footnote on this topic, treat ALL employees as having high potential. People tend to rise to meet expectations, so expect the best and celebrate. As people take pride in their work and in their awareness of your support, everyone wins.

5. I tried it and it failed. That is a reason managers often offer for why delegating failed. Like anything else in life where we fail, it is a matter of taking the time to learn the basics, applying them and monitoring feedback to do it better. Do you swim? The same steps of learning apply: after learning to float, you learned to paddle, and as you learned new strokes, you learned better ways to breathe, and how to improve the results of each stroke. That applies to learning to delegate as well. First, learn the basics and then apply them.

Delegating 101

Delegating is a matter of practice. Let's follow a tutorial session with the Perfect Manager:

Our young manager paused listlessly at the Perfect Manager's office door. "Ma'am. are you available for a few minutes?" he begged. "I'm overworked and need some advice. Lately, I've been working late every night to keep my work unit moving forward. There's just too much work and I"m hoping you have some tips."

Looking up from her desk, the Perfect Manager was clearly annoyed. "Let me understand this. You come to my office, seeking just 'a few minutes', and then describe a problem that could take hours to resolve. Did I get that right? Yes, I have a few minutes to spare, but not enough time now to help you resolve this problem. However, I do have some time tomorrow at 10 am. Does that work for you?"

Feeling embarrassed, the young manager quickly agreed to the proposed time. Remembering that other managers weren't immediately available for his questions was proving a difficult lesson to master. As he turned to leave, the Perfect Manager quipped, "I know you're still struggling with management issues, but I advise you to not seek help from others by implying it will take 'just a few minutes' of the other's time. Instead, acknowledge that the topic is complex, so the other person can respond appropriately. Now, scoot, and I'll see you tomorrow."

Meeting the next morning, the Perfect Manager immediately broached the issue. "So, you mentioned yesterday that you work late every night. My question to you is whether the employees in your work unit work late also, or go home at a regular time?"

Taken aback by this line of questioning, the young manager contended, "Maybe I didn't explain myself. The employees have no problem with their work. I'm the one who is feeling overworked, not them."

"And that's the problem," she patiently explained. "You're trying to do the new responsibilities of management and also continue doing the tasks you did before your promotion. You need to delegate some of that to your team so there is a balance of the workload, and so they will develop bigger roles in their work. Until you start delegating, you're going to continue working those long nights."

"But, but, but...," the young manager stammered. "They don't know how to do some of those tasks, it takes time to train and explain the issues, and I can probably do them faster by doing them myself. I like your idea, Ma'am, but that won't work unless my team are all trained and know the responsibilities. I guess I'll just—"

"Continue working nights," the Perfect Manager interrupted, attempting to hide her frustration. "If you expect to ever get control of your destiny, learning to delegate is vital. Take this one step at a time, working with one assignment to delegate at a time.

"First, identify those responsibilities that must remain yours. Those are the manager tasks to build the organization, improve productivity, reduce costs, or whatever increases value to the corporation. Those must remain with you. These rarely have specific details and are rarely short-term.

"Next, review all remaining work, which should be the majority of what you're doing today, and consider which employee is best suited to learn and execute each assignment. Keep in mind their education and experience and any observed interests.

"Now, from the list, sort them based on the risk of failure. You need to be sensitive to that, as some of those you may want to keep to yourself, but for the others, know that you will want periodic feedback and reviews to keep the assignment moving smoothly.

"At this point, you have a rough outline on how you might reapportion the work. Before taking action, do a careful review on whether the selected employees have the time and define what extra training they will need. These are the basics to start: identifying your responsibilities, defining assignments to delegate, and assessing risk. Do you feel comfortable with that?" the Perfect Manager suggested.

The young manager was now more composed, seeing that delegation was within his grasp. Struggling for words, he responded, "Thank you. Yes, I can do that. Separating the work that way will prevent my delegating that which must remain with me. And if I remove myself from some of the other assignments, I will be able to regain control of my time. But what are the next steps? Do I just hand out the assignments and hope for the best?"

The Perfect Manager smiled; the young manager was getting the message and she saw her time was being well spent in this discussion. "No, no, no," was her reply, shaking her head. "Treat each delegation separately, meeting with the individual to explain the outcome you want, not the mechanics of what to do. In delegation, the individual needs freedom to be creative, so long as the outcome is being achieved. As a check, let the person paraphrase back to you what you want and correct as needed.

"Next, establish a framework for the delegation, such as periodic meetings or status reports, a desired time frame, including what support the individual may need. For example, if the individual will be dealing with people who expected to be working with you, then an introductory letter or phone call should be done to open the communications for the individual. Be sure you both are comfortable with the arrangements and be sure to emphasize the positive aspects of the assignment. Be sure also that you give the support needed.

"From this point, you need to keep up to date on progress, but not meddle in the details. And avoid any tendency to give instructions. You may have suggestions or observations, but your goal is to realize the outcome, not manage the details. The individual is managing the assignment, not you."

The Perfect Manager looked at her clock, noting she had another commitment, so she summarized briefly, "That's pretty much it. Describe the outcome desired, create a framework for the delegation that keeps you current on status, and move forward from there. Got it?"

The young manager seemed relieved, starting to relax as he confirmed, "Yes, I can do this. I see I have work to do and I sincerely appreciate your time. Thank you."

"I'm glad for you," the Perfect Manager concluded. "Here are a few tips: keep communications open, get bad news early, provide needed authority to achieve the assignment, and never delegate to other than those accountable to you. Now, scoot. I need to prepare for my next meeting."

Mastering delegation takes practice. Within a few months, you will feel comfortable with this and will wonder how managers can do otherwise.

david shelby kirk

"The single biggest problem in communication is the illusion that it has taken place" – George Bernard Shaw

Why Are You Hiding?

This chapter is short, but worth a discussion. I'm talking here about the manager's office or cubicle. If you're like 99% of managers, you have a desk toward the back of the office, facing the door. Hiding from the world. Yes, hiding. Sitting with your back to the wall, able to observe immediately when anyone enters your space is appropriate if you need the reassurance of having an obstacle (such as a desk) protecting you from visitors (or if you expect to be physically attacked, but I hope that isn't likely). That desk arrangement may be fine if you need to project your power and authority to all who enter, but is that really your goal?

Who comes your way, anyway? My guess is that your visitors consist mostly of your boss and your team members. You cannot project power and authority to your boss; do you really want to project that image to your team? Or do you want to be approachable? No, you cannot have it both ways if you're hiding behind a desk.

Throughout this book, my focus has been on communicating, so let's see how to make your office more accommodating to that desire. If possible, I suggest placing your desk against a side wall. That ensures your back doesn't face the entrance, yet also frees you from hiding behind it. The first thing you will notice is that your office now has more ROOM. Without that desk where it was, you can now walk around a bit. Okay, maybe your office/cubicle isn't very big, but it will still be bigger after the move.

That guest chair can now be placed slightly away from the desk, allowing you to move your legs from behind the desk and face guests while talking. What does that do? It creates amazing results. One of the first observations is that you and your guest are now closer physically, inviting a more open discussion on topics, partly because both you and your guess are no longer separated by a barrier (your desk).

If you happen to have an office with sufficient space, my next suggestion is to acquire a small round table that will comfortably support two cups of coffee and a couple of notepads and an additional chair. Nothing big. This can be your conversation area and can create the image of a barrier, small though it is.

A conversation area, when possible, should be at least a few feet from your desk. That allows you, when entertaining someone where you wish a bit of formality, to stand when they arrive and move to the small table to sit. This is useful also when there are several people present. Having two areas to converse, one at your desk and one slightly away from it, puts you in full control of how you wish to communicate and how you wish to be viewed.

Whether you have the option for two areas or not, if you follow this suggestion, you will no longer be hidden and you will be viewed by your team as being approachable, which was (I hope) your goal. Good luck.

Quick note: If you do not work in a traditional office environment, but are in an open work environment, you still have challenges in finding opportunities for personal discussion, but you already have an excellent communications environment. Most of my experiences have been in traditional work environments, but I respect and acknowledge that some companies are moving away from that, facing new opportunities and new challenges/problems.

"People who enjoy meetings should not be in charge of anything." - Thomas Sowell

Meetings and You

The word *meeting* is one of management's four-letter words and for good reason. View any manager's calendar and you will likely see it overloaded with meetings to attend. Staff meetings, team meetings, information meetings, and project meetings can all fill your days such that you achieve little else. You become an absentee manager, unavailable for routine interaction with your team.

Unfortunately, you may have little control on some of those meetings. If your superior likes to hold weekly or monthly status meetings of everyone, you're doomed to be there. For some of those information and project meetings, the earlier chapter on delegation may ease the demands for your time.

But it is not just the time; it is whether anything is being accomplished. From my experience, most meetings have no substantive agenda, no specified objective, and no minutes of action items. Without those three, you have a meaningless use of time.

I found years ago that, if I must attend meetings, I shall write my own minutes. In doing so, I call them notes, not minutes, to avoid competing for the role of being the meeting secretary. I send these personal, informal, notes to all attendees after a meeting, always including a comment that there may be substantive omissions or errors and corrections are welcome.

This allowed me to write my understanding of what the meeting was to achieve and who took assignments from the meeting. In doing this, my notes generally became the roadmap of future meetings. That improved focus of the meeting and caused attendees to see me as a valued contributor, influencing the outcome.

Doing this also was a means of confirming that most meetings are really undocumented committees. Yes, my actions were assertive and not always welcome, but assertiveness is vital if a meeting is to avoid dissolving into a tar pit of no goal and no escape.

That strategy works with meetings not under your control, but the meetings where you are the initiator need a different, more open, approach. (And that prevents any attendee from using my strategy, mentioned above.) Before scheduling a meeting, I suggest considering these steps first:

1. Confirm whether anyone cares about the issue. There's always the possibility you're just chasing down a rabbit hole. Do talk to a few associates to gain their views first.

2. Do you need more information from others before proceeding with a meeting? Or can you just move forward and send a memo announcing the direction without a meeting?

3. Do you have a clear idea of the goal, or are you just hoping to present an idea and solicit suggestions (from people who don't know what you want to achieve)? Be careful here. That's thin ice and you can fall quickly.

4. Does the issue require face-to-face discussion at this time, or would a memo requesting others' concerns be adequate at this time?

5. Do the people you plan to invite have a stake in the outcome?

In scheduling the meeting, be sure to write a clear statement of the objective, known issues, and the desired outcome. If you anticipate that several meetings are needed, clarify the agenda and desired outcome for each meeting prior to the meeting itself. This ensures that all participants always know the meeting's purpose. At meeting's end, write your own brief minutes and send to all participants. Retain control throughout.

An alternative approach: *The Committee of One*. I have always believed that a "committee of one gets things done." This is an excellent opportunity for delegation. Consider appointing one person to investigate the issue, and notify those who would have been invited that your appointee will be meeting or discussing or otherwise gathering their contributions that will be collected into a final recommendation. The benefit of this is that each participant gets full attention to their contribution and you have one person to turn to for status. And this is an excellent growth opportunity for a subordinate. This doesn't work for all issues that may need a meeting/committee, but I believe the approach works for many.

Staff Meetings - Yours

Your staff meetings (or team meetings) are a different animal. These serve to build team identity, provide the opportunity for group discussion and other communications, and need to be scheduled often enough to be valued, yet not so often as to cause employees to see them as a waste of time. Yes, it is a delicate line to walk. Much of this is due to your actions: on the one hand, your encourage them to "get things' done", and on the other hand, you schedule meetings that they see as keeping them from doing that.

To fix that dichotomy, you need to adjust the message you send to them, adding that team communications are a part of "getting things done." I also encourage supporting open discussion, which may include complaints, criticisms of upper management or HR policies, and anything else that concerns them. People may hesitate to tell you of their fears or concerns in private, but among their peers they may feel more confidence. And they need this ability to speak as much as you need to hear it. Remember, a large part of your job is LISTENING.

Remember; your employees may have a long history of attending meaningless staff meetings. Turning their perception around may take months.

For the meeting itself:

- Always have something to tell them that they don't know.

- Never apologize for corporate policy. It weakens you.

- Always have part of the meeting for status among the team(s).

- Periodically invite a guest speaker, possibly from another department or function.

- Always allot time for issues and questions.

Do you supervise a group where you need status daily, such as when fielding customer support problems? Something you might consider is a stand up meeting. I had the pleasure of consulting with such an organization, and was invited to attend their daily status meeting. The employees assembled in the hall with their status notes, and within 10 minutes each had shared status of their support tickets, identified where additional support was needed, and secured sign off where appropriate. Just 10 minutes. And then they immediately dispersed. I interviewed a few of the people later: they all confirmed that the daily meeting was productive, saved time, and kept them informed on their colleagues' activities. Definitely, this technique was a a win for them. Would it work for you? Something to consider if the work environment fits.

Okay, that's a wrap for meetings. They can be a curse or useful. You can't control them all, but you can influence all of them to your objectives.

david shelby kirk

"Reading is to the mind what exercise is to the body." - Joseph Addison

Further Reading

No book is ever enough to give you the information to become competent in a profession. In writing this book my focus was on defining the basics on creating and sustaining a productive work environment, but striving to become a perfect manager is a continuing process and I recommend you continue reading management-oriented books throughout your career.

If you aspire to senior management, then continual reading is a *must*. Books on management techniques, such as this one, do not address the issues that senior management faces, especially regarding expanding the vision for a large enterprise and staying abreast of political and economic issues that affect your organization. My philosophy is to *always* have a book you're reading. If not a habit already, make it one.

There are many excellent books and resources available, and everyone has their favorites. These four classics are mine. They reflect the core of management and people, and I have read and reread each of them for years for the insight they offer. My recommendation to you is not just to read them, but to own them. Why? Because to be effective you need key resources always at hand. Together with this book, they form an excellent foundation.

The Effective Executive, by Peter Drucker. My first encounter with this book was in the early 70s at a management workshop. The book's focus could be summarized as "Do the right things", but it is so much more. Building a team that works well together, paying them fairly, and establishing a positive work environment are all excellent objectives, but ineffective if your company would be better served by focusing elsewhere. Managing your time and making the right decisions are two of the most important traits of successful managers. Once you read this book, you'll read it again.

The Peter Principle: Why Things Always Go Wrong, by Lawrence J. Peter and Raymond Hull. Read this book and you will never view people in authority positions the same. And it may confirm what you have inwardly suspected for years. Further, it may help you decide where you want to be within an organization and whether you want that next promotion.

Why Things Go Wrong: Or, The Peter Principle Revisited, by Lawrence J. Peter. This complements the prior book, building and expanding on the topic. Well worth the read, and quite entertaining, as well.

The Dilbert Principle: A Cubicle's-Eye View of Bosses, Meetings, Management Fads & Other Workplace Afflictions, by Scott Adams. You were there once. Remember? Don't lose sight of how you viewed management. This book will remind you.

david shelby kirk

About the Author

David Shelby Kirk has worked in the business world for over forty-five years, with titles of Systems Engineer, Director of Training, Computer Systems Manager, Principal Consultant, Director of Methodologies, and Associate Director of Computing Management.

He is the author of a number of books on computing and has authored articles in several national magazines, including *Computerworld*, *Enterprise Systems Journal*, *Data Training*, and *The Journal of Information Management*. He has also been the key speaker at a number of computing seminars. He and his wife Linda live in Central New York.

You can follow David's writings in his blog at www.davidsplace.org.

david shelby kirk